DRUGS AND ALCOHOL IN THE WORKPLACE

Legal Developments and Management Strategies

Victor Schachter
Thomas E. Geidt
Susan Grody Ruben

Schachter, Kristoff, Ross, Sprague & Curiale
San Francisco

Executive Enterprises Publications Co., Inc.

This publication is designed to provide accurate and authoritative information regarding its subject matter. It is sold with the understanding that the publisher is not engaged in rendering legal, accounting, or other professional service. If legal advice or other expert assistance is required, the services of a competent professional person should be sought. — <u>From a Declaration of Principles jointly adopted by a Committee of the American Bar Association and a Committee of Publishers.</u>

Second Printing

ISBN 0-88057-544-1
Library of Congress Catalog Card No. 86-080565

Printed in the United States of America

DRUGS AND ALCOHOL IN THE WORKPLACE:
LEGAL DEVELOPMENTS AND MANAGEMENT STRATEGIES

TABLE OF CONTENTS

Page

PREFACE i

ACKNOWLEDGEMENTS iv

ABOUT THE AUTHORS v

CHAPTER 1: INVESTIGATIVE TECHNIQUES — BALANCING
THE EMPLOYER'S NEED TO KNOW WITH THE EMPLOYEE'S
RIGHT TO PRIVACY 1

   Constitutional Search And Seizure Rules 1

      U.S. Constitution 1

      State Constitutions 2

   Constitutional Privacy Provisions 2

      U.S. Constitution 2

      State Constitutions 3

   Investigatory Techniques 3

      Observing And Questioning Employees 4

      Collection Of Business Records 5

      Surveillance 6

      Undercover Agents 7

      Polygraphs And Related Devices 7

      Searches 9

   Footnotes – Chapter 1 10

CHAPTER 2: DRUG TESTING 11

   Testing Methods 12

Employee Concerns 13

Legal Parameters 14

    Public Sector 14

    Private Sector 17

Random Testing 21

Bargaining Requirements 23

Other Considerations 26

Recommendations 26

Footnotes – Chapter 2 29

**CHAPTER 3: LIABILITY FOR WRONGFUL DISCHARGE AND
RELATED CIVIL TORTS** 31

Substance Abuse And Job Performance 31

Disciplining Employees For Violation Of Drug
  And Alcohol Rules 32

    "Zero Tolerance" Rules 34

Related Torts 35

    Defamation 36

    Intentional Infliction Of Emotional Distress 38

    False Imprisonment 40

    Invasion Of Privacy 41

Summary 42

Footnotes – Chapter 3 44

**CHAPTER 4: SUBSTANCE ABUSE ISSUES ARISING UNDER
COLLECTIVE BARGAINING AGREEMENTS** 45

The Duty To Bargain 45

How Arbitrators Handle Substance Abuse Cases 47

Drug Cases 48

    Standards Of Proof 48

    Off-Duty Drug-Related Conduct 51

    Investigative Measures 52

Alcohol Cases 52

Discipline Versus Rehabilitation 53

Footnotes - Chapter 4 57

CHAPTER 5: EQUAL EMPLOYMENT OPPORTUNITY LAWS 59

Chemical Dependency As A Protected "Handicap" 59

The Duty To Provide "Reasonable Accommodation" 61

Title VII - Disparate Impact On Minorities 64

Summary 65

Footnotes - Chapter 5 66

CHAPTER 6: STATE BENEFITS LAWS 67

New Theories Of Workers' Compensation Liability 67

Unemployment Compensation Benefits 70

Footnotes - Chapter 6 73

CHAPTER 7: SAFETY IN THE WORKPLACE — PROTECTING CO-WORKERS
AND OTHERS AGAINST SUBSTANCE ABUSERS 74

Footnotes - Chapter 7 77

CHAPTER 8: CORPORATE STRATEGIES TO CONTROL
SUBSTANCE ABUSE 78

Ascertaining The Facts 78

Corporate Commitment 79

Developing A Policy 79

Administering Discipline 80

Sensitivity To Employees' Rights
Of Privacy And Dignity.. 81

Training Supervisors 82

Employee Education 83

Relations With The Union 83

Conclusion.. 83

APPENDIX

Sample Substance Abuse Policy Statement 86

Sample Employee Handbook Policies 87

Checklist Of Substance Abuse Symptoms 90

Excerpts From San Francisco Ordinance......................... 91

Proposed California Drug Testing Law
(Senate Bill No. 2175) 93

Proposed California Drug Testing Law
(Assembly Bill No. 4242) 98

McDonell v. Hunter Decision................................... 104

Shoemaker v. Handel Decision 117

PREFACE

Substance abuse in the workplace is now recognized as a monumental problem. Employee-assistance professionals, psychologists, labor lawyers, and others knowledgeable about drug and alcohol abuse agree that the problem has reached crisis proportions. Chemical dependency is not limited to high-powered, intensely competitive industries, nor is it confined to big cities or specific socioeconomic groups. Every profession, every occupation, every level in the labor-management hierarchy, and every region of the country is affected.

The costs of alcohol and drug abuse are astronomical. In human terms they include lost jobs, morale problems, injuries, illnesses, and deaths. In economic terms they include property damage, employee theft, tardiness, absenteeism, lost productivity, quality control problems, increased health insurance costs, increased workers' compensation costs, and the cost of replacing and training new employees. Recent studies have estimated the nationwide cost of drug abuse to employers to be as much as $60 billion a year.

An increasing number of employers are taking steps to combat drug and alcohol abuse in the workplace. Investigative measures include chemical testing of applicants' and employees' blood or urine, polygraph testing, searches, video surveillance, undercover personnel, and drug-sniffing dogs. The use of these techniques raises novel and difficult legal issues relating to employee privacy, particularly in view of the potential criminal consequences of drug involvement.

Medical and personnel experts differ over whether the primary emphasis in dealing with substance abusers should be on rehabilitation or discipline. Employers have been uncertain whether to discharge substance abusers or to try to rehabilitate them. As the problem magnifies, many employers are opting for a tougher approach toward substance abusers that does not necessarily abandon traditional concepts of rehabilitation, but gives employees an early ultimatum that they must rehabilitate or face termination. This is the approach recommended by many experts.

At the same time, the recent emergence of "wrongful discharge" lawsuits in many states has restricted employers' free reign to discipline employees who violate company drug and alcohol rules. The prospect of a large jury verdict if a discharge is found to violate standards of "just cause" for termination, or an implied duty of "good faith and fair dealing," requires that employers exercise great care in the handling of such cases. Employees disciplined for substance abuse are also using state and federal handicap-discrimination statutes to challenge disciplinary action.

As a result of these developments, employers must simultaneously engage in several difficult and delicate balancing acts. First, they must select investigative techniques that will be effective and reliable, yet will avoid the creation of a "police state" atmosphere. Second, in deciding how to deal with identified abusers, they must walk the fine line between rehabilitation and discipline. Finally, they must weigh the need for discipline against the risks of costly litigation or arbitration. This book identifies key legal issues, explores investigative techniques available to employers, addresses issues raised by rehabilitation and discipline, and describes corporate strategies that can be implemented to control substance abuse in the workplace.

The authors hope that this modest effort to clarify the issues, and to suggest practical approaches to deal with these issues, will help employers to more successfully control substance abuse in the workplace.

Victor Schachter
Thomas E. Geidt
Susan Grody Ruben

San Francisco, California

<u>ACKNOWLEDGEMENTS</u>

In preparing a publication about employment laws that are subject to many varying interpretations, it is inevitable that the final product reflects not only the thinking of the authors, but also of others whose specialized knowledge was invaluable.

The authors would like to acknowledge their gratitude to their partners and associates, whose insights provided a rich resource for each of the chapters.

We also want to thank Fran Fossan and Raila Michelson for their efforts in preparing the manuscript for this book, with its many modifications.

ABOUT THE AUTHORS

SCHACHTER, KRISTOFF, ROSS, SPRAGUE & CURIALE is a law firm engaged exclusively in the practice of labor relations and employment law and litigation representing employers. From its San Francisco office, the firm represents clients in a broad range of fields throughout the United States. In addition to an extensive litigation practice, SKRSC emphasizes preventive steps that can be taken to minimize liability and avoid litigation.

VICTOR SCHACHTER, a partner in the firm, has practiced labor and employment law before federal and state courts, the NLRB, EEOC, OFCCP and other federal, state and municipal agencies. He has served as an attorney with the National Labor Relations Board. Mr. Schachter has written articles in employment law publications and spoken widely before management and legal groups. He is a member of the California and New York bars, the San Francisco Bar Association, the American Bar Association (Labor Law Section and its Committee on Practice and Procedure Before the National Labor Relations Board), and the Lawyers Committee of the American Electronics Association.

THOMAS E. GEIDT, a partner in the firm, has practiced labor and employment law before federal and state courts, the NLRB, EEOC and other federal and state agencies. He has served as an attorney with the National Labor Relations Board. Mr. Geidt has written and spoken extensively on the subject of substance abuse in the workplace. He is a member of the California and Wisconsin bars and the American Bar Association (Litigation Section).

SUSAN GRODY RUBEN, an associate in the firm, works primarily on wrongful discharge, wage and hour, and other employment-related matters before administrative agencies and the courts. She is a member of the California Bar, and the Labor Law sections of the San Francisco, California, and American Bar Associations. Ms. Ruben is the Chairperson of the Bar Association of San Francisco Alternative Dispute Resolution Committee.

CHAPTER 1

INVESTIGATIVE TECHNIQUES — BALANCING THE EMPLOYER'S NEED TO KNOW WITH THE EMPLOYEE'S RIGHT TO PRIVACY

A central issue in drug and alcohol cases is employee privacy. In recent years there has been a surge of interest in employee privacy rights, attributable in part to the technological advances brought about by the computer and other sophisticated methods of collecting and processing information. This has resulted in a proliferation of new state laws that restrict employers' rights to obtain, use, and disclose information about employees. In addition, more employees are seeking court relief under federal and state constitutional provisions.

This chapter will discuss the governing legal principles and several of the investigative methods being used by employers to detect substance abuse. In the next chapter, drug testing, another widely used investigative approach, will be discussed.

Constitutional Search And Seizure Rules

U.S. Constitution

The Fourth Amendment to the United States Constitution guarantees the right to be free from "unreasonable searches and seizures." Whether a search violates the Fourth Amendment turns on whether the area searched is one in which the individual had a "reasonable expectation of privacy." [1] This federal constitutional prohibition, however, controls only <u>government</u> conduct. Unless an employer is acting as an agent of the government, it is not bound by Fourth Amendment principles.

1

Accordingly, private sector employers have great latitude with regard to searches. However, if an employer participates in a search at the direction of law enforcement officers, the employer can be deemed an agent of the government, and federal constitutional protections will be triggered. 2/ A drug "bust" conducted by police authorities, but on company property and with employer cooperation, can also raise federal constitutional search and seizure issues.

State Constitutions

Many state constitutions contain provisions similar to the federal Fourth Amendment search and seizure rule. The reasonable-expectation-of-privacy test is also used in applying these state constitutional provisions to evaluate the propriety of searches. Just like the U.S. Constitution, these state constitutional search and seizure rules apply only to government action.

Constitutional Privacy Provisions

Constitutional privacy rules require that there be a "compelling interest" to justify an invasion of privacy. 3/ Since substance abuse in the workplace is becoming recognized as a huge nationwide problem, courts are beginning to hold that employers indeed have such a compelling interest.

U.S. Constitution

The U.S. Constitution does not expressly provide for the right of privacy, but the Supreme Court has recognized that the Bill of Rights serves as a "penumbra" from which the right of privacy can be implied. 4/ This federal right of privacy has not yet been applied to the context of alcohol and drugs in employment. However, the Supreme Court has held that employees have a privacy interest in their personnel files. The Court upheld an employer's refusal to honor a union's request for individual results of psychological testing done on employees, since the union's desire for such information was not sufficiently compelling to override the employees' right of privacy. 5/

State Constitutions

Some state constitutions have specific provisions regarding privacy. For example, California's constitution, Article I, Section 1, guarantees all Californians the "inalienable right of privacy." In a case interpreting the California constitutional right to privacy, the California Supreme Court held that this right does not protect an individual's right to possess or use marijuana at home. 6/ Accordingly, this constitutional right to privacy would not conflict with an employer's rule prohibiting unlawful drugs at work, since the employer is protecting its "compelling interest" in conducting business safely and productively. However, the California provision has been interpreted as granting employees a right to bring a lawsuit for damages if their reasonable expectation of privacy is breached. As will be discussed in Chapters 2 and 3, state constitutional provisions may significantly affect the rights and liabilities of employers in dealing with substance abuse issues.

Investigatory Techniques

No federal or state constitutional provision precludes employers from investigating and enforcing rules pertaining to drugs and alcohol. Employers have

4

a broad legal right to investigate suspected violations of legitimate rules, and employees have a corresponding duty to cooperate in such investigations.

Employers are using a variety of information-gathering techniques in their campaigns against substance abuse. Methods to monitor the workplace and investigate substance abuse are becoming more sophisticated and effective. With advancing technology comes an elevated concern for employee privacy rights. To help strike a proper balance between the right of employees to be free from overly intrusive surveillance and an employer's need to observe workers and gather information about the "hidden problem" of substance abuse, several approaches are considered below.

Observing And Questioning Employees

The most basic and least intrusive technique of investigating workplace substance abuse is to interview employees who have been observed violating a company rule, or who are suspected of violating such a rule. Interviewing, when done properly, can be an employer's safest and most effective tool in maintaining an orderly workplace.

Interviewing, however, is not free from legal pitfalls. Improperly conducted interviews can result in claims of invasion of privacy. To avoid violating constitutional privacy provisions, employers should conduct interviews in a sensitive, but firm manner, directly presenting the accused employee with the facts and allowing an opportunity for explanation. Newly discovered facts should be investigated before a final determination is made. Interviewers should ask only business-related questions to avoid invading the employee's personal privacy.

Confidentiality should be preserved to the fullest extent possible, and unnecessary publication avoided.

Questioning job applicants about drug or alcohol use should also be done with care. Privacy laws in over a dozen states, as well as many state and federal equal employment laws, prohibit employers from asking applicants whether they have ever been arrested for drug-related (or any other) offenses. Ordinarily, information about drug convictions may be obtained, although some states restrict inquiries about misdemeanor convictions. Massachusetts, for example, prohibits inquiries regarding misdemeanor convictions that are more than five years old, and California prohibits inquiries about convictions for marijuana possession that are more than two years old.

Claims of false imprisonment may also result when an employee is detained for questioning against his or her will. This is discussed further in Chapter 3.

Collection Of Business Records

Employees obviously have a reasonable expectation that information about their drug or alcohol use, including their participation in a rehabilitation program, will not be unnecessarily disclosed to any third party. Indeed, strict confidentiality is the cornerstone of all employee assistance programs, for without assurances that their participation will be kept confidential, many employees will forego needed treatment. Therefore, employers confronted with problems of substance abuse must be sensitive to employees' rights of privacy and dignity.

Some states have statutes regulating an employer's maintenance and use of medical records. Generally, these statutes limit the use of an employee's medical information to those within the company who have a need to know. In order to assure that medical information regarding an employee remains confidential, it is advisable to segregate such records from other personnel records.

Surveillance

A variety of electronic surveillance devices are available to employers. Use of video cameras to observe employees is legal. However, employers should be careful to use cameras only to accomplish a legitimate business purpose (e.g., controlling theft of controlled substances from a medical supply room). To avoid interfering with an employee's reasonable expectation of privacy in closed areas, an employer who wishes to visually survey these areas should post notices that such surveillance may take place. Additionally, it is a misdemeanor offense in some states to install two-way mirrors in lounges, bathrooms, fitting rooms or locker rooms.

Electronic eavesdropping is more restricted by law than visual surveillance. The Federal Omnibus Crime Control and Safe Streets Act of 1968, and statutes in about half the states, restrict employers' rights to use electronic eavesdropping devices to intercept employees' conversations, including telephone conversations. Connecticut, for example, has in its eavesdropping statute a provision that specifically prohibits anyone from "intentionally overhearing" or recording a conversation pertaining to employment contract negotiations, unless all parties to the conversation have given their consent. The California Supreme Court has interpreted California's eavesdropping statute as prohibiting persons from even listening in on an extension telephone without the knowledge and consent of all parties to the conversation, if the conversation was intended to be private. 7/

Undercover Agents

The use of undercover agents, whether posing as employees or customers, is generally permissible. A few states prohibit employers from disciplining employees on the basis of an undercover investigator's report unless the employee has first been given a copy of the report or has been given an opportunity to confront the investigator regarding the accusations.

Undercover agents can be extremely effective in detecting substance abuse without running afoul of laws prohibiting eavesdropping or electronic surveillance. If undercover activity is used by an employer, it should be carried out with the utmost confidentiality, and in a manner that minimizes unwarranted intrusions and embarrassment. It is important that employees have the opportunity to respond to the results of undercover investigations and to explain their side of the story. Such safeguards are an important ingredient in conducting a thorough investigation. Moreover, such safeguards help demonstrate an employer's good faith and fairness.

Polygraphs And Related Devices

Polygraphs and other truth verification devices are widely used in both private and public sector employment because of their relative simplicity and low cost. Although widely used, polygraphs remain highly controversial, due to disputes over their reliability and concerns that they unduly intrude upon employees' rights of privacy and dignity.

A proposed federal law, if enacted, would prohibit employers from requiring employees or applicants to submit to a lie detector test as a condition of employment, and would prohibit employers from using the results of a test for any purpose. Employers would also be prohibited from discharging or otherwise disciplining employees for refusing to take a polygraph test.

Many states already have laws restricting polygraph use by employers. In a majority of states, employees may not be required to take a polygraph test as a condition of becoming or remaining employed; however, testing is permitted if it is strictly voluntary. Some state laws limit the questions that may be asked in a polygraph examination. Nevada, for example, prohibits questions regarding an individual's religion, political affiliations, union affiliations, or sexual activities, unless those affiliations or activities relate to the issue being investigated and the individual being examined has requested that those inquiries be made.

Employers' use of polygraph tests has spawned considerable litigation in recent years and resulted in several large jury verdicts. For example, in one recent case, a supervisor in a New Hampshire restaurant was suspected of using cocaine at work, took a polygraph test, and was discharged based on the test results. He sued for wrongful discharge, invasion of privacy, and defamation, alleging, among other things, that he had been coerced into taking the polygraph test under threat of discharge. He also alleged that he was asked questions by the polygraph examiner that involved personal and confidential matters unrelated to the matter under investigation. A jury awarded him $448,000 on his invasion of privacy and defamation claims, and the award was upheld by a U.S. Court of Appeals. 8/

Searches

Regular exit-and-entry searches and other types of periodic or random searches made by a private employer are generally permissible if conducted for a legitimate purpose and pursuant to a well-defined rule or policy that has been communicated to all employees in advance. Likewise, where there is reasonable cause to believe that an employee is in possession of drugs or other contraband, an employer may normally ask employees to reveal the contents of their pockets, purses, desks, lockers, or other containers, and even their automobiles, when the employees are on company property.

Employees should not be physically touched without their consent; a non-consensual search of an employee's pockets or clothing may constitute assault and battery. However, if an employee refuses to cooperate with a reasonable search request, this is ordinarily grounds for discipline.

10

FOOTNOTES

CHAPTER 1

1. Katz v. U.S., 389 U.S. 347, 360 (1967).

2. See U.S. v. McGreevy, 652 F.2d 849 (9th Cir. 1981).

3. See, e.g., White v. Davis, 13 Cal.3d 757 (1975).

4. Griswold v. Connecticut, 381 U.S. 479 (1965).

5. Detroit Edison Co. v. NLRB, 440 U.S. 301 (1979).

6. National Organization for Reform of Marijuana Laws v. Gain, 100 Cal.App.3d 586 (1979).

7. Ribas v. Clark, 38 Cal.3d 355 (1985).

8. O'Brien v. Papa Gino's of America, Inc., 780 F.2d 1067 (1st Cir. 1986).

CHAPTER 2

DRUG TESTING

Without a doubt, the drug and alcohol issue that has generated the most interest, attention and controversy in recent years is that of chemical drug testing. Many employers have implemented programs requiring job applicants to undergo urinalysis testing for the presence of illegal drugs. A growing number of employers are also requiring existing employees to be tested under certain circumstances. Surveys indicate that between 1982 and 1985, the percentage of Fortune 500 companies screening employees or job applicants for drug use rose from three percent to thirty percent.

Employers are turning to drug testing for a number of reasons. Their increasing awareness of the seriousness of the substance abuse problem has led them to consider all available means of combating the problem. Traditional means of detecting substance abuse — in particular, supervisors' day-to-day observation of employees' behavior — are inherently ineffective where, as is so often the case, employees are able to conceal their involvement in drug-related transactions or their use of drugs on the job. The discipline of employees based on suspicious behavior is often difficult to sustain in the event of a grievance or legal challenge. Given these considerations, together with the natural tendency of most substance abusers to vehemently deny the existence of a problem, it is easy to see why the existence of an objectively verifiable method for determining whether there is a measurable level of drugs or alcohol in an employee's system is a highly attractive prospect for employers.

12

For most enlightened employers, the chief value of drug testing is not that it will make possible the sporadic discharge of employees who test positively for drugs, but that it will have an overall deterrent effect on the use and abuse of drugs among the workforce. Also, it will facilitate early identification of substance abusers and thereby enhance the prospects for rehabilitation.

Testing Methods

There are several types of chemical tests designed to determine the presence of drugs or alcohol in a person's bodily system. The most frequently used test is the Enzyme Multiplied Immunoassay Technique (EMIT) test. This is a urine test that is able to determine whether particular substances are present in a urine sample at a detectable level. The test does not measure the amount of the particular drug that is present, nor does it determine when the drug was used. Depending on the dose taken, most drugs can be detected in a urine sample by the EMIT system for up to two or three days after they have been used. However, marijuana may be detected for as long as two to three weeks. Thus, a positive test result does not necessarily mean that an employee was "impaired" in the performance of his or her job.

Another urine test is the so-called Gas Chromatography/Mass Spectrometry (GC/MS) test. This also determines the existence or non-existence of particular drugs in a person's system, as opposed to the amount of each drug that is present. The GC/MS test is more sophisticated and more expensive than the EMIT test, and is generally used by employers as a means of confirming a positive test result obtained by the EMIT method.

Blood specimens may also be used to determine alcohol or drug usage, including the level of a particular substance in the employee's bloodstream. Thus, blood testing comes closer to measuring "impairment," although the quantity of a particular drug that causes impairment is a matter of scientific debate and may vary from one individual to another.

Breathalyzer tests are another available means of measuring blood-alcohol level. Saliva, brain waves and even hair samples are capable of revealing the presence or absence of alcohol or drugs. The technology of chemical testing is developing rapidly, as efforts are being continually directed toward maximizing the accuracy of the tests and attaining a cost-efficient means of measuring job impairment.

Employee Concerns

As is evident from the massive media attention surrounding this subject, drug testing has sparked considerable controversy and has been opposed by civil liberties organizations, some (but not all) labor organizations, and others. Opponents of drug testing have raised concerns about employees' privacy rights and about the reliability or accuracy of test results. It is argued that drug testing constitutes an invasion of privacy for several reasons: that testing may detect off-duty or "recreational" drug use that has not caused job impairment; that it may reveal other medical conditions, such as pregnancy or AIDS, that could be used by employers for ulterior purposes; and, that where an employee has to be observed while giving a urine specimen, this is itself a privacy intrusion.

Drug testing opponents also cite as a danger that employees may be unfairly discharged or stigmatized by inaccurate or "false positive" test results. It is widely accepted that urine tests may, at times, produce "false positives," particularly if proper testing methods and laboratory procedures are not scrupulously followed.

In addition, opponents of drug testing argue that, because of the potential criminal consequences of illegal drug use, an employee's submission to a drug test creates the potential for self-incrimination, because of the possibility that the test results may be divulged — under subpoena or otherwise — to law enforcement authorities.

To one degree or another, these are legitimate concerns that can and should be addressed by employers.

Legal Parameters

Based on the concerns outlined above, legal challenges to drug testing have been mounted throughout the country. At present, the legal parameters are very much unclear. However, some principles are beginning to emerge from the early cases that have issued.

Public Sector

Almost all of the significant court decisions on drug testing to date have come from public sector employment. Public employers are governed by a stricter legal standard than are private employers, for, as discussed above, they must adhere to the prohibition in the Fourth Amendment of the U.S. Constitution against "unreasonable searches and seizures," as well as the other "due process" protections contained in the U.S. Constitution. Drug testing of public employees has been held to constitute a "search" within the meaning of the Fourth

Amendment, and thus a drug test by a public employer must constitute a "reasonable" search in order to be valid.

In predicting how courts will resolve the legality of drug testing in private employment, it is instructive to consider how they have dealt with the cases that have arisen under the stricter public sector standard. The majority of court decisions so far have upheld drug testing by public employers, especially in safety-sensitive positions, so long as certain standards are met. In one of the first such cases, a federal appeals court held in 1976 that the Chicago Transit Authority's rule requiring bus and train operators to submit to drug testing whenever they are involved in a serious accident or are suspected of being intoxicated or under the influence of narcotics while on duty, was constitutional under the Fourth Amendment. 1/ In 1985, a Georgia federal court upheld the right of a city to require employees whose jobs included hazardous work performed on high voltage wires to submit to drug tests, where the city had a reasonable basis to believe that the employees were using drugs on the job. 2/

In another 1985 case, a District of Columbia court upheld the District's policy requiring police officers to submit to drug testing upon "suspicion" of drug abuse, in view of the dangers and public safety interests involved in police work, so long as the suspicion was grounded on a "reasonable, objective basis." 3/

In 1986, a federal appeals court in Philadelphia upheld a New Jersey state agency's requirement that jockeys who perform in that state's racetracks undergo daily breathalyzer testing and random urine testing. According to the court, the policy was justified by the highly regulated nature of the horseracing industry and the need to ensure the integrity of that industry. 4/

Several other courts, however, have found certain drug testing policies to be constitutionally defective. A federal court in Iowa ruled in 1985 that the Iowa Department of Corrections' drug testing policy violated the Fourth Amendment because it contained no clear standards as to when employees would be tested and gave prison officials unfettered discretion to require such testing. According to the court, drug testing would be permissible only where there is a "reasonable suspicion" based on objective facts that an employee is then under the influence of alcohol or drugs. The court also ruled, however, that testing of job applicants would be constitutional, as would testing done in conjunction with periodic physical examinations routinely required of existing employees. 5/

A state court in Florida held in 1985 that a city's policy authorizing random testing of police officers and firefighters was unconstitutional under the Fourth Amendment. In its decision, the court suggested that the city could test police officers or firefighters only if it had a "reasonable suspicion," based on specific objective facts and rational inferences, that they had violated the city's substance abuse policy. The court characterized "reasonable suspicion" as "something less than probable cause, but something more than a mere suspicion." 6/

In 1986, a federal court in the District of Columbia overturned the discharge of a school district employee based on an unconfirmed positive urinalysis test using the EMIT method. The test had been conducted as part of a generalized program requiring all school system employees to be tested, and not because of any particularized suspicion that the plaintiff had ever used or worked under the influence of drugs. The employee in question was employed as a school bus attendant, assisting handicapped students in getting on and off buses. Thus, according to the court, no public safety considerations justified the city's requirement that she undergo the drug test. 7/

Finally, a federal judge in New Jersey enjoined the City of Plainfield, New Jersey on constitutional grounds from further implementation of its program of testing firefighters and police officers. In that case, the city conducted surprise urinalysis tests of all its current firefighters early one morning, without giving them any forewarning. Sixteen of the firefighters were immediately terminated as a result of unconfirmed positive tests. The terminated employees were not told what substance was found in their urine, given copies of the lab reports or given any opportunity to explain or rebut the results. Prior to conducting the tests, the city had no knowledge or information that any of its firefighters was under the influence of drugs. 8/

Thus, in the cases in which drug testing programs were found to be unconstitutional, the municipalities or agencies involved had generally failed to take the necessary precautions to ensure that employees' privacy and due-process rights were respected. In virtually all of the public sector cases, the drug testing was either upheld as constitutional, or the court indicated that the testing would have been upheld if more limited in scope and/or if more safeguards had been included in the testing programs, such as those discussed at the end of this chapter.

Private Sector

For employers in the private sector, the absence of a Fourth Amendment requirement means that drug testing is unlawful only if it runs afoul of a federal or state law, a local ordinance, a state constitutional provision, or a court-created (common law) theory of liability.

To date, there are no federal or state laws that specifically regulate drug testing in private employment. 9/ Proposed laws have been introduced in several states that would have prohibited or permitted drug testing under various circumstances, but none has yet been enacted. The City of San Francisco enacted an ordinance in 1985 prohibiting any public or private employer from requiring an employee to undergo a drug or alcohol test, except where the employer has "reasonable grounds to believe that an employee's faculties are impaired on the job, and the employee is in a position where such an impairment presents a clear and present danger to the physical safety of the employee, another employee or to a member of the public." All random or company-wide testing is prohibited by the ordinance. However, testing is allowed if agreed to in a collective bargaining contract. Testing of job applicants is also allowed. 10/ Although San Francisco's is apparently the only ordinance of its kind, it is reasonable to expect that other state laws and local ordinances pertaining to drug testing will be enacted in the near future.

Very few states have constitutional provisions that might be interpreted to restrict private-sector drug testing. California, however, is a notable exception. As discussed above, its Article I, Section 1, enacted in 1972, guarantees all citizens the "right of privacy." This clause has been broadly interpreted by the courts and has been held to give employees a right to sue for damages in both the public and private sectors. A 1986 decision of the California Supreme Court involving polygraph testing strongly suggests, without specifically holding, that Article I, Section 1 prohibits most polygraph testing in employment. 11/

Employee lawsuits are pending in California in which drug testing policies are also alleged to violate Article I, Section 1. 12/ The unresolved issue is whether, and under what circumstances, the arguable privacy intrusion is outweighed by a compelling business need.

The kinds of common-law court theories that employees have begun to raise in drug testing situations — and are likely to continue raising in the future — include defamation, intentional infliction of emotional distress, negligence, tortious invasion of privacy, and wrongful discharge in breach of the implied covenant of good faith and fair dealing. (See the discussion in Chapter 3.)

Taking guidance from the principles discussed above, the legal boundaries of drug testing in private employment, although far from clear, may be summarized as follows. First, it appears to be fairly well established that employers have the right to require applicants or prospective employees to undergo drug tests, despite the lack of a particularized suspicion that the applicant is a drug user. Although it has been suggested that the systematic exclusion of applicants who are drug users may constitute a violation of federal or state handicap-discrimination laws, such an argument is unlikely to prevail, since a positive drug test cannot be equated with an addiction to drugs or alcohol within the meaning of the handicap-discrimination laws. (See the discussion in Chapter 5.)

As for existing employees, the early case law suggests that drug testing by private employers is lawful in at least the following circumstances, assuming that proper safeguards are taken to minimize the intrusion into employees' privacy interests:

(1) where there is a "reasonable suspicion" that an employee is impaired or affected by alcohol or drug usage on the job;

(2)   where a drug test is taken in conjunction with a physical examination that may be required of employees on an annual or periodic basis;

(3)   where testing is done as part of a rehabilitation or employee assistance program, or a disciplinary disposition (for example, where an employee is on probation due to a previous positive drug test); and

(4)   where testing is conducted in accordance with the terms of a collective bargaining agreement.

Although it is difficult to articulate all the situations that may constitute a "reasonable suspicion," they would seem to encompass a wide variety of situations, including, for example, where an employee exhibits odd or lethargic behavior, is involved in an accident, makes unexplained mistakes, or experiences a noticeable decline in performance or attendance. (See Checklist of Substance Abuse Symptoms in Appendix.)

If the circumstances justify requiring a drug test, then an employee's refusal to submit to a test would ordinarily constitute an act of insubordination justifying discipline. This is illustrated by a 1986 federal court decision arising in Georgia. The plaintiff, an Atlanta firefighter, was suspected of purchasing marijuana from a co-worker. The plaintiff was asked to submit to a urinalysis test, but he refused. He was suspended, and ultimately terminated, for his refusal to submit to the test. He brought suit, alleging violation of his constitutional rights and invasion of privacy. The court dismissed his lawsuit, holding that the suspected use of drugs by firefighters is a sufficiently rational justification for the requirement that they submit to urinalysis tests. Therefore, even under the strict constitutional standard, his refusal to take the test constituted good and sufficient grounds for termination. 13/

Random Testing

The legality of universal or "random" drug testing — that is, spot tests done on a classification-wide or company-wide basis without any particularized suspicion that the employees being tested are impaired — presents a much closer and more difficult question. A related issue, also unresolved, is whether an employer has the legal right to insist on a "drug-free" or so-called "zero tolerance" environment — i.e., to take action against an employee on the basis of a positive urine test indicating that a particular substance is present in one's system, without a showing that the employee was actually impaired while on the job. Courts in a number of states, including California, have held that an employee may not ordinarily be discharged on the basis of off-the-job behavior unless it is shown that such behavior presents a safety hazard or is otherwise detrimental to the company's operations. 14/

A strong argument for the legality of random drug testing exists where employees work in hazardous jobs or jobs involving significant public safety interests. The need to regulate off-duty drug usage in such safety-sensitive occupations is bolstered by a recent Stanford University study indicating that persons may experience impairment from the use of marijuana and other drugs for longer times than had previously been thought, without perceiving that they are impaired. In the study, ten experienced airline pilots performed simulated landings on computerized equipment designed for pilot performance research. After the first set of simulated landings, each smoked one marijuana cigarette. Twenty-four hours later, when they performed another set of simulated landings, the pilots showed significant impairment from the marijuana smoked a day earlier. Even more disconcerting, the pilots reported no awareness of impaired performance. 15/

Several judges and arbitrators have suggested in their decisions that, in certain occupations, an employee's off-duty use of drugs may be legitimately prohibited or restricted by employers. A Florida appellate court ruled that it would be constitutional for a city to adopt a policy prohibiting police officers and firefighters from using controlled substances at any time, whether on or off the job. According to the court, "the nature of a police officer's or firefighter's duties involves so much potential danger to both the employee and to the general public as to give the city legitimate concern that these employees not be users of controlled substances." 16/

Likewise, a federal appeals court in Denver upheld the discharge of a Union Pacific locomotive engineer who was arrested and later pled guilty to possession of cocaine. The employee was discharged for "conduct unbecoming to an employee" and for violation of the railroad's "Rule 700," which provided that "employees will not be retained . . . who are careless of the safety of themselves or others . . . or who do not conduct themselves in such a manner that the railroad will not be subjected to criticism and loss of good will, or who do not meet their personal obligations." The discharge was upheld by the National Railroad Adjustment Board and later by the federal appeals court, even though the conduct for which the employee was arrested occurred while he was off duty and away from the railroad's property. 17/

Similarly, in March 1986, an arbitrator denied the grievances of two correctional officers employed in a New York prison who were discharged following their off-duty arrests and convictions for possession of drugs. The arbitrator aptly wrote:

> Correction Officers are law enforcement officials . . . .
> Grievants' conduct . . . was and is in direct conflict with the
> duties and responsibilities of a CO . . . . The state has
> proven a direct and substantial relationship between the off-
> duty conduct and their job duties, justifying the imposition
> of discipline . . . . Some things may "go better with Coke"
> but a Correction Officer's job is not one of them. 18/

In non-safety-sensitive situations, however, employers are likely to encounter judicial opposition to random drug testing unless they can show a compelling business need, such as, for example, proof that they have experienced widespread problems of employee drug or alcohol abuse that have adversely affected their operations.

It is likely that court decisions will be issued in the near future that will provide guidance for employers on these complex issues.

Bargaining Requirements

A threshold legal question for unionized employers is whether they owe a duty to bargain with their employees' collective bargaining representative before implementing a drug testing program. This issue has not been squarely resolved by the National Labor Relations Board or the courts. As a matter of general labor law principles, a unionized employer is ordinarily prohibited from unilaterally implementing new rules or procedures affecting employees' working conditions, if violation of the rules may result in discharge or discipline. Safety rules, among other types, have been specifically held to be a mandatory subject of bargaining. Thus, it appears likely that employers will be held to a general duty to discuss and bargain with the union about the implementation of a drug testing program, even if the program is instituted for safety or rehabilitative purposes.

An exception to this general rule exists where the applicable collective bargaining contract contains a broad "management rights" clause or other contractual language which, together with the bargaining history and past practice, indicates that the union has voluntarily waived its right to engage in mid-contract bargaining over the implementation of new safety or work rules. Such a determination was made in 1986, for example, by an arbitrator who upheld the right of a shipbuilding company, Bath Iron Works, to unilaterally implement a comprehensive drug testing program affecting its 7,000 employees. The arbitrator reasoned that the policy did not constitute a "substantial or significant departure" from pre-existing or continuing company rules. 19/

A similar rationale was reached in October 1986, by the U.S. Court of Appeals for the Eighth Circuit in St. Louis in a case arising under the Railway Labor Act. Burlington Northern Railroad unilaterally implemented a drug testing policy permitting it to test employees (1) upon reasonable suspicion of drug or alcohol impairment, (2) following an accident (even without a suspicion of drug impairment), and (3) as part of employees' annual or periodic physical examinations. A federal lawsuit was brought by the union that represents Burlington's employees, alleging that the drug testing policy was a major change in the employees' working conditions so as to require bargaining with the union. However, the U.S. Appeals Court dismissed the union's suit, holding that the drug testing program was merely a "refinement" of the former policy under which the railroad relied on the sensory observations of supervisors to detect violations of its drug and alcohol rules. The court held:

[I]n the past no further testing or detection was necessary once a supervisor had determined through observation that all was not well with the employee. What the railroad has done now is to add a more refined step, the urine test, to confirm the observation of the supervisor. Since the test can be required only upon some showing that the employee may be impaired, the ground rules between the union and the railroad have not changed significantly; suspicion of impairment is still required; instead of simply taking the suspected employee out of service, the railroad now seeks to confirm its suspicion before taking that step. We find no error in the conclusion of the District Court that this amounts, at the most, to only a minor change in working conditions.

Likewise, the addition of the drug screen to Burlington's regular medical examination was deemed a "minor" change not requiring bargaining. The court reasoned as follows:

It is beyond dispute the drug screen is a new technique; the underlying purpose of the medical examinations, however, remain the same — to insure all BN employees are fit for duty. A drug screen is nothing more than a method designed to detect the presence of a newly emerging threat to that fitness.

The use of a more comprehensive urine test has not significantly changed the ground rules between BN and the union. It should come as no surprise to the parties that the components of a work fitness medical examination will change with the times. 20/

On the other hand, several courts have granted preliminary injunctions against employers' implementation of drug testing programs pending collective bargaining with the union or arbitration of union grievances against the testing program. 21/ Thus, the scope of a unionized employer's bargaining duty with respect to drug testing has not yet been fully clarified by the NLRB and the courts.

26

Other Considerations

Employers who are considering drug testing programs must, of course, consider not only the legal ramifications, but also many other practical considerations. The reaction of the employees and the likely impact of a drug testing program on employee morale must be assessed. In this regard, although many employees have strong objections to drug testing for one reason or another, a number of employers have discovered that employee morale was actually enhanced by a tough approach to employee substance abuse. Most employees do not want to risk their safety, or to cover for the mistakes and performance problems of fellow employees who are impaired by drugs or alcohol.

Other practical considerations include which testing methods and laboratory procedures to use, how best to announce a testing program to employees, how to ensure that supervisors and managers are properly implementing the policy, when employees should be tested, who in management needs to authorize or approve the giving of a test, and what action to take in the event of a positive test result. On the latter point, each employer must decide whether its emphasis will be on rehabilitation or discipline, or some balance of the two. To the extent the emphasis is on rehabilitation, the acceptability of the program among employees, as well as its legality, are likely to be enhanced.

Recommendations

Because of both the legal and practical nuances and complexities, it is important that employers undertaking drug testing programs do so with much care and forethought, and with sensitivity to employees' legitimate privacy concerns. The following recommendations are designed to minimize potential legal risks and enhance employee acceptability of any drug testing program that may be implemented.

(1) Clear, advance written notice should be given to employees of the company's drug testing policy and its rules pertaining to drugs and alcohol.

(2) The selection of persons to be tested should not be left to arbitrary considerations, nor have a disparate impact upon minorities.

(3) Written consent forms should be obtained from employees or applicants who are to be tested.

(4) The tests should be processed only by reliable, certified laboratories, with due regard for proper chain-of-custody procedures.

(5) Back-up, confirming tests should be conducted, preferably by a different testing method, when the initial tests are positive. This does not mean that a second blood or urine specimen needs to be obtained; the confirming test can be conducted on the initial specimen. With respect to testing of job applicants, as distinct from employees, it is not imperative that confirming tests be conducted, although it is desirable in the interests of fairness.

(6) Test results should be kept strictly confidential, and not divulged to anyone inside or outside the company who does not have a legitimate business need to know the information.

(7) Employees should be afforded an opportunity to explain or rebut positive test results, or to internally appeal any disciplinary action taken on the basis of a test result.

(8) Positive test samples should be retained for a reasonable period of time in cases where employees are disciplined as a result of a drug test.

(9) Supervisors should be well trained on how to properly implement and administer the policy.

(10) A company's policy should apply across the board to everyone at all levels in the company, management and rank-and-file alike.

(11) Employees whose confirmed test results are positive, and who are willing to undergo some form of rehabilitation or counseling, should ordinarily be afforded that opportunity before being terminated, especially if they are long-term employees.

FOOTNOTES

CHAPTER 2

1. Division 241 Almagamated Transit Union (AFL-CIO) v. Suscy, 538 F.2d 1264 (7th Cir. 1976).

2. Allen v. City of Marietta, 601 F.Supp. 482 (N.D.Ga. 1985).

3. Turner v. Fraternal Order of Police, ___ F.2d ___, 120 LRRM 3294 (D.C. Cir. 1985).

4. Shoemaker v. Handel, 795 F.2d 1136 (3d Cir. 1986).

5. McDonell v. Hunter, 612 F.Supp. 1122 (S.D. Iowa 1985).

6. City of Palm Bay v. Bauman, 475 So.2d 1322 (Fla. 1985).

7. Jones v. McKenzie, 628 F.Supp. 1500 (D.D.C. 1986).

8. Capua v. The City of Plainfield, ___ F.Supp. ___ (D.N.J. 1986).

9. The only exception is an Oregon statute that prohibits breathalyzer testing, except where an employer has "reasonable grounds to believe that the individual is under the influence of intoxicating liquor."

10. San Francisco Ordinance No. 97-85-44, enacted November 1, 1985.

11. Long Beach City Employees Association v. City of Long Beach, 227 Cal.Rptr. 90 (1986).

12. E.g., Luck v. Southern Pacific Transportation Co., et al., San Francisco Superior Court No. 843230 (1985), involving a computer programmer who was terminated for refusing to submit to a urine test pursuant to the employer's company-wide testing program.

13. Everett v. Napper, 632 F.Supp. 1481 (N.D.Ga. 1986).

14. E.g., Rulon-Miller v. International Business Machines Corporation, 208 Cal.Rptr. 524 (1984).

15. "Carry-Over Effects of Marijuana Intoxication on Aircraft Pilot Performance: A Preliminary Report," American Journal of Psychiatry, 142:1325-1329 (1985).

16. City of Palm Bay v. Bauman, supra, note 6.

17. Watts v. Union Pacific Railroad Co., 796 F.2d 1240 (10th Cir. 1986).

30

18. New York Department of Correctional Services, 87 Lab.Arb. 165 (Babiskin, 1986).

19. Reported in BNA Daily Labor Report (July 29, 1986).

20. Brotherhood of Maintenance of Way Employees, Lodge 16 v. Burlington Northern Railroad Co., __ F.2d __ (8th Cir. 1986).

21. Murray v. Brooklyn Union Gas Co., 122 LRRM 2057 (N.Y. Sup. Ct. 1986).

CHAPTER 3

LIABILITY FOR WRONGFUL DISCHARGE
AND RELATED CIVIL TORTS

Traditionally, private employers in the U.S. have had the legal right to discharge employees "at will." The increasingly popular doctrine of wrongful discharge, however, is eroding this traditional right. Under the new theories, courts may find that certain discharges breach an express or implied employment contract, breach an implied covenant of good faith, or violate public policy. This new body of wrongful discharge law has placed limits on employers' absolute rights to discipline suspected drug or alcohol abusers and makes it imperative that employers understand how they may rightfully discharge employees without incurring liability.

Even in those states where wrongful discharge theories are most broadly construed, employers still have the right, as a general rule, to discipline employees if (1) their use of drugs or alcohol impairs their ability to properly perform the job, or (2) they use drugs or alcohol on the job or on company premises in violation of a rule specifically prohibiting such use.

Substance Abuse And Job Performance

One of the most basic managerial prerogatives is an employer's right to evaluate the performance of its employees. It is an employer's right to establish performance and attendance standards for all employees and to take appropriate disciplinary action against those who do not meet the standards, for whatever underlying reason. Employees are not insulated from discipline if their performance problems are attributable to the use of drugs or alcohol, except to the extent that, in certain circumstances, an employee's dependency on drugs or alcohol constitutes a protected "handicap" entitling the employee to reasonable accommodation, as discussed in Chapter 5.

Where a good worker exhibits an unexplainable decline in performance or attendance, this may be attributable to drugs or alcohol or other personal problems. Although experts differ, most agree that it is not a supervisor's proper function to delve into employees' personal problems or to attempt to diagnose their physical or mental conditions. Rather, they should focus on performance. However, supervisors should also be trained to spot warning signs indicating that substance abuse or other personal problems may be the cause of performance problems and, in such cases, without delving into the particulars, refer such employees to resources for employee assistance. Employees who refuse to obtain assistance for their problems may be held to the same standards as all other employees and may be terminated if their performance does not meet standards.

In implementing discipline, employers should ensure that employees be put clearly on notice of the standards expected of them and of the problem areas needing correction, and that employees be given a fair opportunity to take the necessary corrective action before being terminated.

Disciplining Employee For Violation Of Drug And Alcohol Rules

As will be explored further in Chapter 4, the evolving law of wrongful discharge derives much of its approach to "just cause" from arbitral definitions of just cause under union contracts. Accordingly, central to any corporate response to substance abuse is notice of the work rules prohibiting drugs and alcohol in the workplace. In addition to notice, just cause normally requires an adequate investigation of the violation, consistency in enforcement of the rules, and progressive discipline, where appropriate. These four elements are useful not only to unionized employers, but to all employers, because they form the basis for traditional notions of fairness and "due process" in the employment context.

It is critical that employers establish rules that clearly indicate to employees what conduct is proscribed. These rules should be widely publicized. Each employer must decide what kinds of rules and policies regarding substance abuse it wishes to promulgate, taking into consideration its "corporate culture" and other circumstances.

It is not advisable to rely solely on generalized "good conduct" rules, such as "employees are expected to conduct themselves in a safe, legal and considerate manner while at work," or "you may be disciplined for engaging in any conduct unbecoming an employee of XYZ Corporation." Where drugs or alcohol are concerned, such generalized rules may not be sufficient to satisfy the requirement of notice implicit in wrongful discharge and arbitral law. Instead, rules should normally cover at least the following areas:

- use, possession, sale, or solicitation of illegal drugs during the workday or on company property;

- unauthorized use of alcohol during the workday or on company property; and

- reporting to work under the influence of alcohol or drugs.

Some sample drug and alcohol rules are found in the Appendix.

In addition, the rules should be consistently enforced. If violations of the rules are often condoned or "winked at," later attempts to take disciplinary action may not hold up in court or in an arbitration. If, as has been true for many employers, enforcement of drug and alcohol rules have been historically lax, but an employer wishes to toughen its enforcement of the rules, it should notify all employees of this intended change in advance, so that they are forewarned.

"Zero Tolerance" Rules

Some employers have adopted strict policies requiring that all employees be completely free of alcohol or drugs while at work — that is, that there be <u>no</u> noticeable level of alcohol or drugs in their bodily systems. Under such policies, a positive urine or blood test showing the presence of prohibited substances is deemed to be grounds for removal from the job pending rehabilitation or, in the alternative, discharge.

These "zero tolerance" policies are controversial, for their practical effect is to restrict to some extent employees' off-duty use of drugs, since some drugs remain detectable in a person's body for more than a day (and in the case of marijuana, for more than a week) after being used.

The legality of this kind of policy has not yet been determined. As discussed in Chapter 2 in regard to drug testing, some courts have suggested that employers — even those governed by a strict Fourth Amendment standard — may establish zero-tolerance policies, even if it restricts off-duty drug use, with respect to employees who occupy positions affecting public health and safety, such as law enforcement officers, air traffic controllers, airline pilots and motor vehicle operators.

However, it is far from clear whether employees who do not occupy such safety-sensitive positions may be discplined under a zero-tolerance rule. Such discipline is likely to spawn litigation, at least until employers' rights in this area become clearer. For example, a California lawsuit, pending as of this writing, is illustrative. The suit stemmed from a 1985 incident in which Southern Pacific Railroad directed 489 of its employees to undertake urine tests as part of a drug and alcohol detection program. One of its computer programmers refused, telling her supervisor that she believed such a test was a violation of her personal rights. After repeatedly refusing to take the test, she was discharged for "failing to comply with instructions of proper authority." She sued for wrongful discharge, among other things, and contends that the drug test was unrelated to her desk job. Southern Pacific, on the other hand, contends that such tests are job-related for employees in all positions. The company cites statistics showing that, during the first year of its companywide drug-testing program, the number of employees who tested positive decreased by nearly one-half, and the number of human-factor accidents, injuries and days lost were sharply reduced. 1/

Employers' rights in this area will remain clouded until guidance emerges from decisions of the courts.

Related Torts

Employees who sue for wrongful discharge often attach other "tort" claims to their suits, such as defamation, invasion of privacy, intentional infliction of emotional distress and negligence. These claims, if sustained, may entitle an employee to recover substantial "emotional distress" damages or punitive damages from a jury. The following are some of the tort claims most commonly found in drug and alcohol cases.

Defamation

If an employee or job applicant is falsely accused of being a drug user and the accusation is communicated to a third party, this may give rise to a defamation claim.

To establish defamation, an employee need only show that a false statement about him or her was communicated to a third person, and that the statement is of a type that would likely harm the employee's reputation or deter other persons from desiring to deal with the employee in the business setting. False statements accusing employees of having committed a crime or having engaged in conduct adversely affecting their fitness to perform their jobs would be defamatory in character. Defamation may be based on a written communication (libel) or an oral statement (slander).

An employer can defend against a defamation claim by establishing either that the statement was true or that it was "privileged." In general, an employer's statement about an employee is privileged if it is communicated for a legitimate business reason to a person who has a reason to know the information. The privilege may be lost, however, if the employee can prove that the statement was made with malice or that the communication was excessive to accomplish the ostensible business purpose — for example, if it was communicated more times or to more persons than was necessary.

These principles are illustrated by a state court case from Texas. 2/ In the case, a railroad switchman was injured on the job and fainted. The company doctor ordered drug screening, which showed positive for a trace of methadone. The doctor reported the presence of the trace to the company personnel officer, adding that "methadone is a drug which is used in treating heroin addicts," but that the trace meant nothing. The personnel officer sent an internal memo to the seven managers who normally received accident reports. The memo stated that methadone had been found in the employee's urine and that methadone was used to treat drug addicts. The memo did not mention that only a meaningless trace was found.

The employee was suspended from work. He had his own doctor run tests, which showed no traces of methadone, and sent this information to his employer. The employee was discharged, not for the use of narcotics, but for violating the employer's safety and accident reporting rules. The employee, a veteran, then contacted the Veterans' Administration regarding his discharge. In the course of investigating the veteran's complaint, the Department of Labor contacted the company. A company personnel officer responded in writing to the Department of Labor, explaining the safety violations that caused the termination and noting that methadone traces were an additional reason for the discharge. The letter made no mention of the insignificance of the test result, nor did the letter mention the contrary test result found by the employee's own doctor.

The employee filed suit, claiming defamation. The jury found that both the internal memo and the letter to the Department of Labor were libelous. It awarded the employee $150,000 in compensatory damages and $50,000 in punitive damages.

In contrast, a federal court in Texas, faced with a different set of facts, took a sympathetic view of an employer's need to investigate substance abuse. 3/ This case involved two unionized employees who worked for an oil company. Both employees were suspected of being drug users. The employees were suspended and required to undergo medical tests. Since the tests on both employees registered negative for drug use, the employees were reinstated.

The employees sued the company on a variety of tort claims, including defamation. The court found that the employees' claims were preempted by the Labor Management Relations Act, that is, that the proper remedy was to take their complaints through the company's and union's grievance procedure. Significantly, the court also commented that it found no basis for the defamation claims. Rather, it found that the company had merely asked the employees reasonable questions to aid in an investigation. The court stated:

> To hold the company guilty of defamation for making such inquiries, even though they become known in the plant, would simply mean that the company could never undertake to investigate a possible disciplinary situation in routine and proper ways, or a possible situation involving physical or mental difficulties of an employee. There was not the slightest evidence . . . that the company in any way tried to cast the employees in an unfavorable light. Whatever references to possible drug use . . . which were made were made in the restricted personnel meetings in which the investigations were proposed and discussed.

Despite this court's sympathetic view of an employer's need to investigate substance abuse, employers would be wise to deal with disciplinary situations in as confidential a manner as possible, restricting information regarding an employee's suspected substance abuse to those who have a need to know such information.

Intentional Infliction Of Emotional Distress

An employer may be liable for intentional infliction of emotional distress if it is found to have engaged in "outrageous" conduct that was done in "reckless disregard" of the probability that it would cause an employee emotional distress, and if the employee, in fact, experiences severe emotional distress as a result of the conduct. Behavior may be considered "outrageous" if the employer (1) abuses its position of authority or power over the employee, (2) knows that the employer is susceptible to injuries through mental distress, or (3) acts intentionally or unreasonably with the recognition that the acts are likely to cause mental distress.

Thus, a wide variety of circumstances could trigger a claim of intentional infliction of emotional distress. An employer who does not give adequate notice to employees of its rules or investigatory procedures (e.g., searches, testing, etc.), could be found liable for intentional infliction of emotional distress during the investigative or disciplinary process. Moreover, an employer could be found liable for intentional infliction of emotional distress if it conducted a test or a search in an unreasonable manner.

For example, an employee in a California case sued for wrongful discharge and intentional infliction of emotional distress. 4/ The employee was a supervisor in a hospital. As part of a general investigation by hospital management concerning drug use by hospital employees, the supervisor was questioned about her use of drugs and her knowledge of drug use by employees in her department. Based on management's finding of substance abuse in her department, she was discharged on the grounds that she had failed to adequately supervise the employees in her department.

The employee's intentional infliction of emotional distress claim was based on her allegations that she was not given an opportunity to defend herself against management's charges and was publicly escorted from the hospital upon being discharged. The court found, however, that the employer's conduct was not extreme or outrageous with the intention of causing, or a reckless disregard for causing, emotional distress. Rather, the court pointed out, if these facts could constitute a claim for intentional infliction of emotional distress, every termination would be accompanied by such a claim. As a result, the court rejected the employee's claim.

The above case is a welcome one for employers, in that it reiterates the concept that a termination, by itself, does not create a cause of action for intentional infliction of emotional distress. The case is a reminder to employers, however, to steer clear of such emotional distress claims by keeping terminations businesslike, private, and free from unnecessary recriminations.

False Imprisonment

The tort of false imprisonment can occur when an individual is intentionally confined or restrained by another person. The following case illustrates this tort in the context of a disciplinary investigation. The case is a primer on how not to conduct an investigation.

An employee suspected of stealing money was taken to a small room lit by a bare bulb and detained by two security officers who accused her of theft and questioned her for one-and-one-half hours. Eventually, the employee agreed to sign a statement admitting the theft. She was then driven by the security officers to her bank, where she withdrew money at their direction. After returning to the employer's place of business, the officers told the employee she still owed money and demanded that she call her relatives to bring money. Otherwise, the officers stated, the employee would be put in jail. The employee sued for false imprisonment and was awarded $25,700 in damages. 5/

41

Although not involving drugs, this case illustrates the problems an employer may have if the manner in which it investigates alleged drug or alcohol use is deemed unreasonable. Clearly, an employer is entitled to conduct an investigation when there is a need. Regarding the tort of false imprisonment, all an employer need avoid is confining an employee against his or her will. If, during an investigatory interview, an employee wishes to leave, the employer should normally allow the employee to do so. However, an employee who wishes to prematurely end an investigatory interview can be told that failure to participate in the investigation will lead to discipline, up to and including termination. Generally, such a policy will encourage even the most recalcitrant employee to remain at the investigatory interview.

Invasion Of Privacy

Invasion of privacy is a common law tort independent of constitutional privacy rights. Thus, even where a state's constitution does not include a separate right to privacy, an employer should still conduct investigations with employee privacy rights in mind.

The tort of invasion of privacy in the employment context can occur when:

(1)   the employer makes a highly objectionable intrusion against an employee's right to be let alone;

(2)   the employer publicly discloses private facts about an employee; or

(3)   the employer puts an employee in a "false light."

These elements are illustrated by a 1984 invasion-of-privacy case from Texas, in which an employee claimed that an unannounced search of her company

42

locker and its contents violated her privacy. The court held that, although the company provided the locker, <u>the employee supplied her own lock, thus evidencing an expectation of privacy.</u> An award of $100,000 in punitive damages for invasion of privacy was upheld. The appellate court suggested, however, that had the employer provided the locks and kept a master key, or clearly notified employees that lockers were subject to search, a different result would have been reached. <u>6</u>/

Thus, employers can maintain their managerial prerogatives regarding searches by maintaining control over company property. If employees are put on notice that lockers, desks, and other such areas are subject to search, an employee no longer has a <u>reasonable</u> expectation of privacy, and the employer is not violating any employee privacy rights if it finds it necessary to conduct a search.

Summary

The law of wrongful discharge and related torts is still evolving, particularly in the substance abuse context. What is already clear, however, is that employers should carefully think out their response to workplace substance abuse, rather than to hastily implement a few work rules, or worse, to discipline employees without any rules in place. Central to any substance abuse policy will be the four steps discussed above: (1) notice to employees of the policy; (2) thorough investigation of suspected violations of the policy, including an opportunity for employees to explain their side of the story; (3) consistent handling of any violations of the policy; and 4) progressive discipline, where appropriate. Moreover, to minimize claims of related torts such as defamation and intentional infliction of emotional distress, discipline for substance abuse should be carried out in as confidential, dignified, and businesslike a manner as possible, given the stigma that is attached to this type of misconduct.

FOOTNOTES

CHAPTER 3

1. Luck v. Southern Pacific Transportation Co., et al., San Francisco Superior Court No. 843230 (1985).

2. Houston Belt & Terminal Railway Co. v. Wherry, 548 S.W.2d 743 (Tex. 1977).

3. Strachan v. Union Oil Co., 768 F.2d 703 (5th Cir. 1985).

4. Santa Monica Hospital v. Superior Court, 172 Cal.App.3d 698, 173 Cal.App.3d 348, 182 Cal.App.3d 878 (1985), rev'w grntd, ___ Cal.3d ___, 222 Cal.Rptr.224 (1986).

5. Black v. Kroger Co., 527 S.W.2d 794 (Tex. 1975).

6. K-Mart Corp., Store No. 7441 v. Trotti, 677 S.W.2d 632 (Tex. 1984).

CHAPTER 4

SUBSTANCE ABUSE ISSUES ARISING UNDER
COLLECTIVE BARGAINING AGREEMENTS

Unionized employers have two additional questions to deal with in the substance abuse area. First, is there a duty to bargain with the union regarding implementation of drug and alcohol rules or policies? Second, under what circumstances does discipline for violation of drug/alcohol rules constitute "just cause," so that it will be sustained in the event of arbitration?

The Duty To Bargain

As mentioned in Chapter 2, unionized employers are required by the National Labor Relations Act to bargain with the union regarding "wages, hours, and other terms and conditions of employment." 1/ Stated differently, if employees are represented by a union or other collective bargaining representative, their employer is generally prohibited by law from changing the employees' wages, hours or working conditions underlyingly — that is, without first bargaining in good faith with the union. Additionally, once a collective bargaining agreement has been executed, employers are obligated to honor the terms of the contract. This obligation is embodied in contract law and in federal labor law.

New drug and alcohol rules carrying disciplinary penalties constitute a "working condition" and are, therefore, normally a mandatory subject of bargaining. When an employer owes a legal duty to bargain over a particular subject, it must meet and confer in "good faith" with the union in an attempt to reach an agreement. The law does not require that an agreement be reached or that an employer make any particular concession or proposal. If, after good faith bargaining, the parties are unable to reach an agreement and instead reach an impasse, the employer is generally permitted under federal labor law principles to unilaterally implement its last offer with respect to the matter in question, unless an existing contractual provision expressly prohibits the employer's action.

Although an employer generally owes a duty to bargain about changes in its work rules, there are several situations in which such a duty will be found not to exist, especially where the union has waived its right to bargain. Such a waiver can arise in a variety of ways. For example, if an employer unilaterally modifies its work rules and the union fails to protest the action or to request bargaining, the union may be deemed to have lost its right to engage in any such bargaining. Similarly, if an employer notifies the union that it is contemplating certain changes in its rules or policies, and indicates, directly or indirectly, its willingness to bargain, but the union takes no action to request bargaining, the union will have waived its bargaining rights.

Alternatively, a union may expressly agree to relinquish its right to bargain about a particular mandatory subject, and embody such an agreement in a contract. For example, if the parties have negotiated a broad "management rights" clause in their contract, expressly permitting the employer to make changes in its work rules, safety policies or the like, this may be tantamount to an agreement that the employer may unilaterally implement a substance abuse policy.

The parties' past practice and bargaining history will normally be relevant in determining whether an existing contract should be interpreted as allowing unilateral implementation of new work rules. If the employer has made similar changes over the years without bargaining, and without a protest from the union, a court or arbitrator would likely find that implementation of a new substance abuse policy is contractually permitted.

Bargaining notes and other evidence of the parties' discussions during their past collective bargaining negotiations may also establish whether a management rights or other clause was intended to permit unilateral implementation of a substance abuse policy. For example, if an employer attempts to negotiate a drug testing program as part of its negotiations for a new collective bargaining agreement and the union refuses to agree to such a clause, the employer will be hard-pressed to argue during mid-term of the contract that its general "management rights" clause permits it to unilaterally implement a drug testing program.

To summarize, although the law in this area is not a model of clarity, unionized employers generally owe a duty to bargain over the implementation of new drug and alcohol policies. That duty, however, is not an onerous one. And, in some instances, the duty may not exist at all.

In any case, it is advisable for employers to seek the cooperation and assistance of unions in combating the problem of employee substance abuse. Unions owe a legal obligation to represent their members fully and fairly in regard to matters affecting their safety, and many unions have shown a willingness to cooperate in the establishment of a strong and effective substance abuse program.

How Arbitrators Handle Substance Abuse Cases

Drug and alcohol cases have been common for many years under grievance-arbitration procedures. Arbitrators appear to handle alcohol abuse cases somewhat differently from drug abuse cases, upholding alcohol-related discharges more often than drug-related discharges.

Drug Cases

One striking fact revealed by a review of the recent arbitrations reported in the Bureau of National Affairs Labor Arbitration Reports is that arbitrators have overturned more drug-related discharges than they have sustained. From March 1980 through January 1985, discharges were sustained in only twenty-one of forty-six cases (excluding those involving the sale of drugs). 2/ Moreover, one arbitrator, in a 1983 opinion, cited his own study of arbitral decisions from 1973 to 1982, in which he found that arbitrators set aside approximately two-thirds of all discharges involving employee possession or use of drugs on company premises. 3/

Standards Of Proof

Ironically, although drug abuse is now recognized as one of society's greatest employment problems, it appears to be difficult for unionized employers to sustain disciplinary action for drug-related conduct. This can be explained partly by the stricter standards of proof applied by arbitrators in drug cases. Ordinarily, an employer need show by only a "preponderance of the evidence" that the events that would support the termination actually occurred. In drug cases, however, arbitrators hold employers to a higher standard of proof. Some arbitrators require employers to establish the employee's guilt of the rule infraction by proof "beyond a reasonable doubt," the same standard applied in criminal trials. Others require that the employer's evidence be "clear and convincing," a standard that is also more stringent than the preponderance-of-the-evidence standard.

The rationale for applying these standards, as presented by arbitrators, is that matters carrying the "stigma" of criminal conduct or of general social disapproval must be applied with an especially high degree of fairness, supported by strong proof. Arbitrators have also noted that an employee discharged for such an offense may have extreme difficulty finding another job, thus making it imperative that the employer be correct in its accusations.

In drug cases, therefore, arbitrators tend to resolve all reasonable doubts in favor of the employee. They also generally require the employer to produce corroborating witnesses to the drug usage, rather than relying on one witness alone. This compounds the employer's difficulties of proof, since, in drug situations, other employees are often particularly reluctant to testify against co-workers.

Thus, of the twenty-five arbitrations previously referred to that were won by employees, over forty percent were decided on the basis that the employer had insufficient evidence to establish the employee's guilt under these strict standards of proof. In another forty percent of the cases, arbitrators found that the employee violated the employer's rules against drug usage, but that the punishment was too severe to fit the crime. In these cases, the arbitrators felt that the employee should be given the opportunity to undergo drug rehabilitation treatment before the termination was finalized. Thus, reinstatement was made contingent upon successful treatment.

The remaining cases won by employees were decided on a variety of grounds. In some instances it was found that the employee did not have adequate notice of the rules. In other cases, the rules were disparately enforced. In at least two cases, arbitrators found that drug use was so widespread at the employer's facilities that the employer in each case was not entitled to "crack down" on drug use without giving employees advance warning of its intention to do so. 4/

In a few cases, discharges were overturned because the employer had not clearly spelled out which substances were prohibited under its posted rules. Finally, the discharge of one employee who admitted selling illegal drugs to other employees was overturned because the employee had been denied his contractual right to have a union steward present during the disciplinary meeting with company representatives. 5/

Even when an employee, while under the influence of drugs, has an accident causing severe property damage, this will not necessarily constitute just cause for termination. For example, an employee of the Chicago Transit Authority was discharged after operating a rapid-transit train in the wrong direction while on drugs. The train collided at high speed with another train, causing massive damage to both trains. Nevertheless, the arbitrator set aside the discharge and ordered the employer to admit the employee into its drug rehabilitation program. The arbitrator concluded that the enormity of the damage was an "irrational and arbitrary standard" upon which to terminate the employee, in view of the existence of an employee assistance program that other employees were ordinarily permitted to enter in lieu of termination. 6/

Even though most drug use is a crime, employers have been singularly unsuccessful in arguing to arbitrators that on-the-job use or possession of drugs should be treated as a more serious contract violation than on-the-job alcohol consumption. Instead, arbitrators have pointed out that some illegal drugs, such as marijuana, have become nearly ubiquitous in our society, that alcohol is still considered the nation's number-one substance abuse problem, and that there is no rational basis to treat the two types of substances differently in the workplace. Therefore, in facilities where alcohol use is widely condoned, arbitrators have generally refused to uphold discharges based on the possession of drugs. 7/

Off-Duty Drug-Related Conduct

Another frequent issue is whether, and under what circumstances, employees may be disciplined for drug-related conduct occurring away from company premises while employees are on their own time. It is a widely accepted principle of arbitral law that what employees do on their own time is their own business and is not an appropriate subject of disciplinary action, unless the conduct could reasonably be said to affect the company's business, reputation, or product; render the employee unable to perform properly the duties of the job; or affect other employees' morale or willingness to work with the employee.

Some arbitrators have recognized that off-duty drug-related conduct, especially where selling is involved, may justify disciplinary action. 8/ Often, however, an employee's arrest or conviction for off-duty possession or use of drugs has not been considered just cause for termination. 9/ Even felony convictions for the off-duty sale or distribution of drugs have been held, in some cases, to be an insufficient basis for termination. On the other hand, if the employer can show a connection between the off-duty incident and the individual's job performance, there is a much higher chance that a discharge in such a context will be upheld, as, for example, where the employee occupies a security-sensitive position or a high-visibility "public relations" position.

Investigative Measures

Finally, arbitrators usually recognize investigative techniques, such as chemical testing, undercover agents, trained dogs, video surveillance, and reasonable searches, as being within management's inherent prerogative, unless, as is rarely the case, these techniques are expressly prohibited by the collective bargaining agreement. Similarly, an employee's refusal to submit to a reasonable search or a chemical test to detect the presence of drugs is generally recognized by arbitrators as an act of insubordination sufficient to sustain disciplinary action, as long as the employer's conduct was reasonable under the circumstances and "due process" procedures were followed. 10/

Alcohol Cases

Interestingly, employers seem to have a greater success rate in arbitrating cases involving employee abuse of alcohol than in arbitrating cases involving drugs. From March 1980 to January 1985, of forty-nine disciplinary cases involving alcohol reported in Labor Arbitration Reports, discipline was upheld in thirty-two cases and overturned in only eighteen. 11/

One possible explanation for the disparity between arbitration decisions in alcohol and drug cases is that drug infractions are more difficult for employers to prove, particularly under the strict standards of proof discussed above. Moreover, employees are more careful to conceal their involvement in drugs, due to the potential criminal consequences. Also, employees will go to greater lengths to contest accusations of drug use, more often retaining their own attorneys to assist them in processing their grievances.

In comparing alcohol and drug arbitrations, there is a noticeable difference in the tenor of the two types of cases. In alcohol-related cases, there are fewer hair-splitting evidentiary battles over the sufficiency of the evidence. In nearly all of the forty-nine alcohol-related cases referred to above, the arbitrators found sufficient evidence that the employees had, in fact, consumed alcohol on the job, reported to work under the influence of alcohol, or allowed their attendance or work performance to suffer as a result of an alcohol problem. In only two of the cases were the discharges set aside based on "insufficient evidence" of a rule violation. 12/

The alcohol cases tend to focus mainly on the severity of the discipline. In sixteen of the eighteen cases won by employees, the arbitrators found discharge to be too severe a punishment, due to a variety of mitigating circumstances. In many of the cases, the employer's disparate or lax enforcement of its substance abuse rules was cited as a factor. In other cases, the absence of prior warnings or the employee's exemplary work history was cited. In one case, similar to a drug-related case discussed above, the discharge was set aside based on a violation of the employee's right to have his union steward present during the disciplinary interview.

Discipline Versus Rehabilitation

In many of the cases examined for this study, the arbitrator believed that the employee's career might be salvaged through rehabilitation. The issue of rehabilitation arises much more frequently in alcohol cases than in drug cases. It is not entirely clear why this is so. There appears, however, to be a greater willingness by arbitrators to recognize that alcohol dependency is a treatable illness than to recognize drug dependency as one. This makes it all the more paradoxical that drug-related discharges are more often nullified than are alcohol-related discharges.

Arbitrators are not of one mind on the issue of discipline versus rehabilitation. Some arbitrators apply traditional principles of progressive discipline even where a condition of alcohol dependency may exist. Sometimes they do so on the rationale that their authority is limited to deciding whether a contract violation occurred, and thus, that they lack authority to order rehabilitation. At other times the arbitrator's explanation is that alcohol abuse is a serious problem, and only through a firm disciplinary approach is it likely that an employee will face up to the problem and modify his or her behavior.

Many other arbitrators believe that extreme leniency should be shown toward employees who may have an alcohol dependency problem. These arbitrators premise this approach on the basis that alcoholism is an illness that renders the employee unable to control his or her own conduct. In a majority of the situations where an employee is willing to acknowledge an alcohol dependency, arbitrators will expect that the employee be given at least some opportunity to receive treatment in the hope that his or her career may be salvaged.

Often, before an employee is terminated, the employer, union, and employee will enter into an agreement that the employee must participate in certain rehabilitation efforts, with the understanding that if the employee drops out of the treatment or is otherwise unsuccessful in curing his or her problems, employment will be terminated. Where the employee violates such a "last-chance" warning or agreement, arbitrators will usually, but not always, uphold the termination.

In a case involving such a "last-chance" agreement, a federal appellate court in Ohio held that an arbitrator acted beyond his authority in setting aside a discharge. 13/ In that case, an employee had an acknowledged drinking problem. On one occasion, he was suspended from work for being intoxicated while on duty. In discussions between the employee and the company, an agreement was worked out whereby the suspension was rescinded in exchange for the employee's agreement to attend Alcoholics Anonymous meetings. The employee subsequently came to work intoxicated on two more occasions. After the second occasion, the employee was again suspended.

The employee's union filed a grievance over the latter suspension. Prior to arbitration, however, the parties worked out an agreement whereby the company rescinded the suspension in exchange for the employee's promise to attend out-patient treatment sessions at a local hospital. This "last-chance" agreement placed the employee on a six-month probationary period and provided that the employee's adherence to the agreement was a condition of continued employment. Specifically, the agreement stated that "failure to comply with [this agreement] or any alcohol related infractions at work will result in dismissal."

Six weeks later, the hospital notified the company that the employee had failed to attend his treatment sessions for the prior two weeks. The company confronted the employee, who responded that he had been having car trouble. The company discharged the employee, in accordance with the "last-chance" agreement. The union grieved the termination. The arbitrator, basing his decision on the employee's "long years of seniority," reinstated the employee on the condition that he try again to adhere to the rehabilitation agreement.

The case ended up in court, where the court agreed with the employer that the original "last-chance" agreement was binding. Since the court found that the employee had violated that agreement by failing to attend his treatment sessions, the court upheld the discharge, finding that the arbitrator had exceeded his authority in disregarding the explicit terms of the parties' settlement agreement.

Occasionally, employees assert at an arbitration hearing that their attendance or performance problems were attributable to a previously undisclosed drinking problem. Although arbitrators will sometimes set aside such a termination pending alcoholism treatment, they more often uphold the disciplinary action, so long as it appears that the employer was not aware of the employee's chemical dependency prior to the termination. 14/

Finally, where no apparent alcohol dependency is involved, but rather, an ordinary violation of company rules against drinking on the job or reporting to work under the influence of alcohol, arbitrators normally apply traditional principles of progressive discipline. Unless the contract explicitly provides to the contrary — and sometimes, even when it does — arbitrators ordinarily will not uphold discipline for a first offense. Among the factors considered by arbitrators in deciding such cases are the clarity of the employer's rules; the consistency of rule enforcement; the type of industry (i.e., whether it is one in which employee alcohol abuse would present special dangers to the public or co-workers); the history of prior warnings; the employee's length of employment and work history; and any other mitigating circumstances that may exist.

FOOTNOTES

CHAPTER 4

1. 29 U.S.C. § 158(d).

2. Discipline was upheld in 74 Lab.Arb. 163, 1012; 75 Lab.Arb. 301, 642, 816; 76 Lab.Arb. 379; 77 Lab.Arb. 721, 1085; 78 Lab.Arb. 545, 749, 753, 921, 1104, 1334; 79 Lab.Arb. 69; 80 Lab.Arb. 419, 1292; 81 Lab.Arb. 174, 1169; 82 Lab.Arb. 558; 83 Lab.Arb. 270.

   Discipline was overturned or reduced in 74 Lab.Arb. 953, 1032, 1103; 75 Lab.Arb. 1081; 76 Lab.Arb. 144, 308; 77 Lab.Arb. 1001; 78 Lab.Arb. 274, 697, 1299, 1309; 79 Lab.Arb. 1185, 1327; 80 Lab.Arb. 663, 1074, 1261, 1292; 81 Lab.Arb. 974, 988; 82 Lab.Arb. 6, 150, 360; 83 Lab.Arb. 580, 635, 680.

3. Mallinckrodt, Inc., 80 Lab.Arb. 1261, 1265 (1983) (Seidman, Arb.).

4. Lockheed Corp., 75 Lab.Arb. 1081 (1980) (Kaufman, Arb.); Watauga Indus., Inc., 78 Lab.Arb. 697 (1982) (Galambos, Arb.).

5. Aeronca, Inc., 71 Lab.Arb. 452 (1978) (Smith, Arb.).

6. Chicago Transit Authority, 80 Lab.Arb. 663 (1983) (Meyers, Arb.).

7. See, e.g., Mallinckrodt, Inc., supra, note 5; Hooker Chemical Co., 74 Lab.Arb. 1032 (1980) (Grant, Arb.).

8. E.g., Martin-Marietta Aerospace, Baltimore Div., 81 Lab.Arb. 695 (1983) (Aronin, Arb.); Group W Cable, Inc., 80 Lab.Arb. 205 (1983) (Chandler, Arb.).

9. E.g., Vulcan Asphalt Refining Co., 78 Lab.Arb. 1311 (1982) (Welch, Arb.).

10. E.g., Mich. Consol. Gas Co., 80 Lab.Arb. 693 (1983) (Keefe, Arb.); Prestige Stamping Co., 74 Lab.Arb. 163 (1980) (Keefe, Arb.).

11. Discipline was upheld in 74 Lab.Arb. 25, 316, 641; 75 Lab.Arb. 699, 899, 901, 968; 76 Lab.Arb. 163, 845, 1178; 77 Lab.Arb. 448, 854, 1052, 1064, 1180; 78 Lab.Arb. 89, 302; 79 Lab.Arb. 182; 80 Lab.Arb. 503, 639, 851, 875; 81 Lab.Arb. 243, 318, 344, 449, 630, 733; 82 Lab.Arb. 420, 861; 83 Lab.Arb. 760.

58

Discipline was set aside or reduced in 74 Lab.Arb. 664, 972; 75 Lab.Arb. 255, 518; 76 Lab.Arb. 758, 1005; 77 Lab.Arb. 289, 775; 78 Lab.Arb. 793, 1060; 79 Lab.Arb. 196, 529; 80 Lab.Arb. 193; 81 Lab.Arb. 917, 1083; 82 Lab.Arb. 31; 83 Lab.Arb. 211. In one other case, 75 Lab.Arb. 1147, the arbitrator upheld the discharge of six employees but set aside the discharge of two others.

12.   Hayes-Albion Corp., 76 Lab.Arb. 1005 (1981) (Kahn, Arb.); General Felt Indus., Inc., 74 Lab.Arb. 972 (1979) (Carnes, Arb.). Even in these two cases, the employees were acknowledged to have been drinking before reporting for work, but it was not demonstrated to the arbitrator's satisfaction that the employees were intoxicated or "unfit" to work. In Hayes-Albion, the employee had consumed approximately twenty-four beers in the early morning, gone home and slept for five hours, and then had reported to work.

13.   Bakers Union Factory No. 326 v. ITT Continental Baking Co., Inc., 749 F.2d 350 (6th Cir. 1984).

14.   E.g., Bemis Co., Inc., 81 Lab.Arb. 733 (1983) (Wright, Arb.); Western Gear Corp., 74 Lab.Arb. 641 (1980) (Sabo, Arb.).

CHAPTER 5

EQUAL EMPLOYMENT OPPORTUNITY LAWS

Chemical Dependency As A Protected "Handicap"

Some courts have held that alcoholism and drug addiction are protected "handicaps" under various federal and state employment-discrimination laws. This means, in essence, that employers who are governed by these laws may not discharge, refuse to hire, or otherwise discriminate against employees because of an alcohol or drug dependency if, after reasonable accommodation is made to their condition, the employees are qualified to perform the job in spite of the handicap.

The federal Rehabilitation Act of 1973 prohibits government contractors and subcontractors from discriminating against "qualified handicapped individuals." A "handicapped individual" is defined in the Rehabilitation Act, 29 U.S.C., Section 706(7)(B), as:

> [A]ny person who (i) has a physical or mental impairment which substantially limits one or more of such person's major life activities, (ii) has a record of such impairment, or (iii) is regarded as having such an impairment....[S]uch term does not include any individual who is an alcoholic or drug abuser whose current use of alcohol or drugs prevents such individual from performing the duties of the job in question or whose employment, by reason of such current alcohol or drug abuse, would constitute a direct threat to property or the safety of others.

The latter sentence was added by Congress in 1978 to make clear that, although alcoholics and drug abusers are "handicapped individuals" for purposes of the Act, employers are not required to employ them if they cannot perform the job properly or if they present a threat to property or safety. Thus, the "Catch-22" for employees is that they must simultaneously prove that they are handicapped by their chemical dependency, but not so handicapped as to be unqualified to perform their job.

The Rehabilitation Act has been enforced in favor of alcohol and drug abusers in a variety of contexts. For example, the City of Philadelphia was found to have violated the Act by maintaining a blanket policy against the hiring of current and former drug abusers. 1/ A college professor who claimed he was denied tenure due to his alcoholism was found to have stated a valid claim under the Act. 2/ In another case, a teacher who alleged that he was harassed, given poor evaluations, and then discharged after disclosing his diagnosis and treatment for alcoholism was also found to have a valid claim. 3/

In addition to the federal Rehabilitation Act, there are laws in most states prohibiting employment discrimination by private-sector employers based on one's handicap. Although the statutes vary from state to state, and relatively few reported cases have arisen under them so far, it is likely that alcoholism and drug addiction are protected "handicaps" under many of those statutes. For example, in a recent Ohio case, an employee of an automobile dealership was experiencing problems due to his use of drugs and alcohol. He requested a one-month leave of absence to obtain care and treatment. In response he was summarily terminated. The Ohio Supreme Court held that drug and alcohol addiction are protected handicaps under Ohio's fair employment law, and the employee's discharge was therefore unlawful. 4/

The California Legislature has taken a different approach, which may be adopted in other states. Although California's handicap-discrimination statute does not cover alcoholism or drug addiction, the state recently enacted an "alcoholic rehabilitation" statute. This law requires all employers having twenty-five or more employees to reasonably accommodate alcoholic employees by giving them the opportunity to take time off from work to enter and participate in an alcoholic rehabilitation program, provided that this does not impose an undue hardship on the employer's operations. 5/ The time taken off by an employee need not be with pay. Employees, however, must be allowed to use their accrued sick leave while participating in an alcoholic rehabilitation program. The law further provides that employers are not prohibited from discharging or refusing to hire employees who, because of their current use of alcohol, are unable to perform their job duties, or would endanger their own safety or the safety of others while performing their duties.

The Duty To Provide "Reasonable Accommodation"

In the context of substance-abuse cases, what exactly does the duty of reasonable accommodation require? Most statutes do not spell out the requirements, and court decisions have yet to shed much light on this subject. The courts have just begun to grapple with this question, mostly in the context of public-sector employment. The U.S. Supreme Court, in its 1986-87 term, has agreed to determine whether a public school teacher's third relapse of tuberculosis was a handicap entitled to reasonable accommodation under the Rehabilitation Act. 6/ The Court's decision in this case may help to shed some light on an employer's duty to reasonably accommodate substance abusers.

One case already decided by a lower federal court is potentially far-reaching in its implications. 7/ The case involved an employee of the U.S. Department of Labor whose alcoholism seriously affected his work performance and caused him to be repeatedly absent from work. His unauthorized absences, which totaled nearly 500 hours during his last year of employment, caused severe problems for his department. His employer took extensive steps over a four-year

62

period to accommodate his condition. The employer permitted him to reduce his hours and offered him a transfer to a less stressful job. It counseled him and referred him to various rehabilitation programs. The employee was hospitalized several times for detoxification treatment, and he participated in a variety of outpatient rehabilitation programs. His problems, however, persisted. After a final warning, the employee was terminated.

Surprisingly, a federal judge found that the employer had not done enough to reasonably accommodate the employee's handicap. According to the court, the employer displayed too much indecision in its handling of the employee's problems, did not give him a "firm choice" between rehabilitation or discipline early enough, and should have given him one more opportunity to rehabilitate himself before terminating his employment.

In another case, a federal judge overturned the discharge of an alcoholic employee of the U.S. Department of Defense who had been repeatedly absent from work. 8/ Prior to his termination, the employee had undergone treatment for his alcoholism. Following the treatment, he was again absent without authorization on several occasions, although the latter absences were unrelated to his alcoholic condition. In discharging him, the employer considered his pre-treatment and post-treatment absences cumulatively. The court ruled that the employer should have forgiven, and not considered at all, the absences that predated the employee's treatment for alcoholism. The court found that, utilizing the employee's "alcohol-induced pretreatment transgressions" as a factor, the employer failed to reasonably accommodate the employee's condition.

Because federal employers are governed by a different set of laws and regulations protecting handicapped workers than are employers in the private sector, the reasonable-accommodation requirements found applicable in the two cases described above are not necessarily coextensive with those binding on private employers. However, these decisions may foreshadow the kinds of measures that will be considered necessary in the private sector.

At minimum, the duty of reasonable accommodation probably requires employers to give employees who are willing to acknowledge a chemical dependency an adequate opportunity to rehabilitate themselves through appropriate employee assistance programs (EAP's) or community resources, unless the granting of such an opportunity would impose an undue hardship on the employer. Presumably, the obligation also requires, as the California law states, that employees be allowed to use their accrued sick leave and disability leave benefits for this purpose. It is unlikely that employers are required to contribute directly to the cost of rehabilitation unless they so choose, except to the extent that their existing EAP's, sick leave or medical insurance benefits may provide for such coverage. Many states have enacted statutes requiring that employers' group health insurance plans include coverage for alcohol and/or drug rehabilitation.

Other possible means of reasonable accommodation may include adjustments in employees' job duties, transfers, and reassignments or scheduling changes designed to alleviate stressful conditions that may be contributing to an employee's chemical dependency.

A 1986 court decision from New Mexico dealt with reasonable accommodation of an employee's drug use in the context of a claim of religious discrimination under Title VII. The plaintiff in the case, a Native American, was a member of a church that occasionally used peyote (an hallucinogenic drug derived from mescaline) several times a year in its religious ceremonies. The church's use

64

of peyote was based on the sincerely-held belief that peyote possesses sacred qualities and is effective in healing certain conditions, including the disease of alcoholism.

The plaintiff applied for a job as a driver of "18-wheel" tractor-trailers. He was told that he would be hired if he passed several tests. In one of the tests, a polygraph exam, he disclosed his infrequent use of peyote. As a result of this disclosure, he was not hired. No attempt was made at first to accommodate his religious use of peyote. Following his filing of an EEOC charge, the company made a settlement offer in which it agreed to pay him back pay and to employ him subject to the following limitations: (1) he could attend peyote ceremonies up to twice a year; (2) he had to give the company a week's advance notice before using peyote; and (3) he had to refrain from working the day after his use of peyote (which would normally be a Sunday, when he was not scheduled to work anyway).

The plaintiff rejected this offer and brought a Title VII action in federal court. The court ruled that the company violated Title VII when it initially rejected the plaintiff's application without making any attempt to accommodate his use of peyote. However, the court further held that the company's subsequent offer constituted a "reasonable accommodation" of the plaintiff's religious drug use. Consequently, because the plaintiff had rejected the offer, his lawsuit was dismissed. 9/

Title VII – Disparate Impact On Minorities

There are essentially two types of discrimination — disparate treatment, where a member of a protected class is treated differently; and disparate impact, where a facially neutral policy impacts a protected class in a harmful way. In several cases, it has been argued that certain employers' policies of rejecting applicants who are methadone users have an adverse impact on Blacks and Hispanics, in violation of Title VII of the Civil Rights Act of 1964.

The U.S. Supreme Court has rejected this argument, however, at least in the context of safety-sensitive jobs. In a case involving the New York City Transit Authority, the Court held that rejecting methadone users was a more precise and less costly policy than alternative policies for screening employable methadone program participants. The Court found that if the City hired any methadone users, even in non-safety jobs, it would have to exert special efforts to obtain reliable information on applicants' methadone program participation, monitor methadone users' progress in the program, and take precautions against their promotion to "safety-sensitive" positions, from which the Court found they could be lawfully excluded. Thus, the Court held that a statistical demonstration of adverse minority impact was overcome by the City's showing of "business necessity." 10/ The U.S. Equal Employment Opportunity Commission ("EEOC") has approved this same "business necessity" analysis. 11/

Summary

Treatment of drug addiction and alcoholism as a protected "handicap" is a growing phenomenon across the country. Employers who contract with the federal government or who operate in states having handicap-discrimination laws protecting substance abusers should be mindful of their duty to provide reasonable accommodation, which includes, at minimum, making a thoughtful analysis of what can be done to accommodate the applicant or employee.

66

FOOTNOTES

CHAPTER 5

1. Davis v. Bucher, 451 F.Supp. 791 (E.D.Pa. 1978).

2. Whitaker v. Bd. of Higher Educ. of the City of New York, 461 F.Supp. 99 (E.D.N.Y. 1978).

3. Athanas v. Bd. of Educ. of School Dist. 111, Highwood-Highland Park, Ill., 28 FEP Cases 569 (N.D.Il. 1980).

4. Hazlett v. Martin Chevrolet, Inc., 25 Ohio St.3d 279 (1986). See also, Conn. Gen. Life Ins. Co. v. Dep't. of Indus., Labor and Human Relations, 273 N.W.2d 206 (Wis. 1979).

5. California Labor Code §§ 1025-28.

6. Arline v. School Board of Nassau County, 772 F.2d 759 (11th Cir. 1985), cert. grntd., __ U.S. __, 106 S.Ct. 1633 (1986).

7. Whitlock v. Donovan, 598 F.Supp. 126 (D.D.C. 1984).

8. Walker v. Weinberger, 600 F.Supp. 757 (D.D.C. 1985).

9. Toledo v. Nobel-Sysco, Inc., __ F.Supp. __, 41 FEP Cases 282 (D.N.M.)

10. New York City Transit Authority v. Beazer, 440 U.S. 568 (1978).

11. EEOC Decision 80-13, 26 FEP Cases 1795 (1980).

CHAPTER 6

STATE BENEFITS LAWS

New Theories Of Workers' Compensation Liability

An obvious result of employee alcohol and drug abuse is an increase in industrial accidents, which, in turn, causes an increase in employer liability for workers' compensation benefits. It has been estimated that substance abusers file five times as many workers' compensation claims as persons who are not so afflicted. Even more ominous for employers is the possibility, under new workers' compensation theories, that employers will bear liability for causing employees to develop alcohol or drug dependency.

For example, the California Workers' Compensation Appeals Board (WCAB) awarded benefits to an employee who claimed he was disabled as a result of a drinking problem that was caused or aggravated by the stresses and strains of his job. 1/ The employee was a nondrinking alcoholic when he started his job as a mailroom clerk. Over the next several years, as the company grew in size, the employee's workload increased. He requested additional staffing, but his employer felt he should be able to handle the job alone. He then started drinking at lunch and after work. His alcohol consumption gradually increased in amount, and he eventually attempted suicide while intoxicated. After a brief hospitalization he returned to work, again became intoxicated, and again was hospitalized. The employee was diagnosed as suffering from depression and organic brain damage that rendered him totally disabled. The WCAB awarded him benefits on the ground that he had suffered an industrial injury — nervous tension — that caused his drinking problem and ultimately caused his total disability. The WCAB's decision was upheld by the courts.

This decision may portend a general recognition of drug and alcohol dependency as "industrial" illnesses — or at least as by-products of compensable industrial stress — thus expanding employees' entitlement to compensation and treatment within the framework of the workers' compensation laws. Under the same rationale, employees who are absent for prolonged periods while seeking drug or alcohol treatment may claim protection from discharge under those state workers' compensation laws that prohibit discrimination or retaliation against employees based on their being industrially injured or disabled. 2/ Generally, an employee whose drug or alcohol problem is classified as a compensable work-related injury will be entitled to return from a medical leave of absence if he or she is competent to perform the job, and the position remains available.

A related issue is whether the emotional stress of being accused of drug-related activities may itself be grounds for recovery of workers' compensation or related benefits. This theory was upheld in a 1983 California Supreme Court case involving a probation officer employed by Los Angeles County. 3/ The employee was investigated for involvement in drug transactions and was ultimately terminated for negotiating a sale of drugs to a federal enforcement agent. He appealed the dismissal, and as a result of various civil service commission and court proceedings, he was ordered reinstated with back pay, apparently because his guilt of the drug infractions was not sufficiently proved. After being reinstated, he worked for approximately another year and then applied for a disability pension, claiming psychiatric disability. The retirement benefits he sought were available only for disabilities that "arose out of employment," the same standard used in workers' compensation proceedings. His claim for the disability benefits was initially denied, but was then appealed to the courts.

A California trial court found that the employee was "psychiatrically incapacitated for work because of stress resulting from the county's unsuccessful attempt to dismiss him for dealing in illegal drugs." The court denied his claim for disability benefits, however, because it found that his disability did not arise out of his employment; rather, it arose out of his termination for alleged off-duty misconduct.

The California Supreme Court reversed. It found that the psychiatric disability was employment-connected. Quoting from the court's decision:

> While illegal conduct in the performance of a job-related act will not preclude a finding that resulting disability is service-connected . . . the present charges if sustained would have established illegal activities wholly unrelated to plaintiff's duties and thus outside the scope of his employment. And for purposes of analysis we assume, without deciding, that had plaintiff been demonstrated to be guilty of those charges, and his termination upheld, he would not be entitled to a disability pension by reason of the resultant stress. But the fact is that the charges were not proved, the purported determination was overturned, and plaintiff was reinstated to his former job with back pay . . . .
>
> We therefore conclude that when an employee is investigated and disciplined by the employer on charges of misconduct that are unproved and therefore presumably false, and the discipline set aside, the resulting psychological stress and injury arises out of and in the course of employment . . . .

Thus, according to the reasoning of this decision, an employee's eligibility for workers' compensation benefits resulting from the psychological stress of being investigated or terminated for a drug-related infraction may hinge on whether the employee's misconduct is ultimately proven in the criminal courts, or otherwise.

These workers' compensation issues are obviously novel, and the courts have not yet squarely resolved them.

Unemployment Compensation Benefits

If an employer discharges an employee for matters relating to drugs or alcohol, the employee's entitlement to unemployment compensation benefits will frequently become an issue. Most states provide unemployment benefits when an employee is discharged, unless the employee was guilty of "willful misconduct." Accordingly, an employee who is discharged for violation of a drug or alcohol rule may receive unemployment benefits if it is determined that the employee's alcoholism or drug addiction caused a non-volitional breach of the work rule, but will not receive benefits if the breach is found to be willful.

For example, in one unemployment case, an employee was discharged due to excessive absenteeism concededly caused by his alcoholism. 4/ The employer argued that the employee should not receive unemployment benefits because his absenteeism constituted willful misconduct. The court disagreed with the employer, holding that the employee's alcoholism was a disease that incapacitated him from controlling his actions, thereby entitling him to benefits.

If, however, an employee violates a drug or alcohol rule, but the employee is not an alcoholic or drug addict, the violation will likely be found to be willful, making the employee ineligible for unemployment benefits. As an example, an employee in Illinois who was discharged for drinking on the job argued that she was entitled to unemployment benefits because her employer had not demonstrated that her alleged misconduct had actually "harmed its interests." 5/ The court rejected the employee's argument and denied the benefits, holding that once misconduct is shown by the employer, there is no need to show that the employer was actually harmed.

Moreover, if an employee with a substance abuse problem agrees to undergo rehabilitation in return for continued employment, it may amount to misconduct if the employee drops out of the treatment program. This principle is illustrated by a New York case where an employee with a drug problem had been discharged for falsifying doctor's notes to justify absences. 6/ Subsequently, however, the employee and the employer worked out an agreement whereby the employee was reinstated for a one-year probationary period in exchange for his promise to attend a year-long outpatient drug abuse treatment program. The employee stopped attending the program after one month and thereby lost his job. His employer argued that he was not entitled to unemployment benefits because his failure to attend the treatment program constituted misconduct. The employee argued that his failure to attend the program was merely "poor judgment," but not misconduct. The court agreed with the employer and denied benefits, holding that the employee's promise to attend the year-long drug treatment program was an "essential" condition of his reemployment. Accordingly, the court found that the employee's failure to sustain rehabilitation amounted to misconduct, thus disqualifying him for unemployment benefits.

In 1986, the State of Oregon's Employment Division adopted a formal policy, the first of its kind in the nation, providing that employees are disqualified for unemployment benefits if they were discharged, or were denied a job with a prospective employer, based on their refusal to submit to a drug test. The Oregon agency adopted the policy in response to a rapid increase in unemployment claims linked to drug tests. According to the agency, fifty claims related to drug tests were processed in August 1986 alone.

Each state has its own standards for granting unemployment benefits. A general proposition appears to be, however, that the "willfulness" of the employee's conduct will be central to a determination of entitlement to benefits. Of course, such a determination is not always readily apparent, given the controversy even in the medical community about the amount of control an individual has over the use of alcohol or drugs once a dependency has developed.

FOOTNOTES

CHAPTER 6

1. California Microwave, Inc. and Pacific Indemnity Co. v. Workers' Compensation Appeals Bd., 45 Cal.Comp.Cas. 125 (1980).

2. See, e.g., California Labor Code § 132a, as interpreted by the California Supreme Court in Judson Steel Corp. v. Workers' Compensation Appeals Bd., 586 P.2d 584 (1978).

3. Traub v. Board of Retirement of the Los Angeles County Employees Retirement Association, 34 Cal.3d 793 (1983).

4. Jacobs v. California Unemployment Insurance Appeals Board, 25 Cal.App.3d 1035 (1972).

5. Jackson v. Board of Review of the Department of Labor, 105 Ill.2d 501 (1985).

6. Matter of Restifo, 452 N.Y.S.2d 690 (1982).

CHAPTER 7

SAFETY IN THE WORKPLACE — PROTECTING CO-WORKERS AND OTHERS AGAINST SUBSTANCE ABUSERS

Under general principles of negligence law, employers have a duty to provide a safe workplace. Moreover, under the Occupational Safety and Health Act (OSHA) and related state safety laws, employers must comply with specific regulations that provide for a safe workplace. Thus, an employer's desire to deal fairly and humanely with employees who have substance abuse problems must be counterbalanced against its duty to protect the safety of employees and others from injuries that may be caused by impaired employees. These competing interests are difficult to reconcile, for the more compassionate or tolerant an employer is in employing someone with a chemical dependency, the more likely it is that an injury or accident will ultimately occur.

For example, a construction employer in New York was found liable when an employee died from an accident caused by alcohol consumption. 1/ The employee's estate sued the employer, claiming that the employer knew of the widespread consumption of alcohol on its construction site. The court held that the employer's failure to take action regarding this situation supported a claim for violation of the employer's duty to provide employees with a safe place to work.

A decision of the Texas Supreme Court further graphically illustrates the dilemma faced by employers. 2/ In that case, a machine operator was discovered to be intoxicated on the job. Recognizing that his condition was a safety hazard, the supervisor sent the employee home early. While escorting the employee to the parking lot, the supervisor asked him if he was all right and if he could make it home. The employee answered that he could. While driving home, the employee had an accident, killing himself and several occupants of another vehicle. He was found to have a blood alcohol content of 0.268 percent. The families of the other victims sued the company for wrongful death.

Employers have traditionally been held vicariously liable for employees' acts committed during employment. In this case, however, the employee was off duty when the accident occurred, and therefore the company could not be held vicariously liable. Instead, the plaintiff's theory was that the company was directly liable to the victims' families because of the supervisor's negligence in failing to control the intoxicated employee.

The court upheld the families' right to bring the suit under this novel theory, saying that it was for the jury to decide whether the company acted negligently in failing to control the actions of the intoxicated employee. The court reasoned that "changing social standards and increasing complexities of human relationships in today's society justify imposing a duty upon an employer to act reasonably when he exercises control over his servants." Thus, the court implied that the supervisor may have had an affirmative duty to restrain the intoxicated employee, even against his will, from leaving the company premises, or to arrange alternate transportation.

Few states impose "dram shop" liability; that is, liability of a bartender or social host who supplies alcohol to a person who, in turn, causes injury to a third person. Nevertheless, employers may face liability to such third persons, even though they, unlike bartenders, did not contribute to or condone the employee's intoxication.

Another illustration of the strict duty, and the resulting dilemma, imposed on employers is a 1986 jury award from Southern California. There, a hospital patient sued a hospital after being sexually assaulted by one of the hospital's orderlies while the patient was recovering from brain surgery. The patient alleged that the hospital was negligent in retaining the orderly as an employee. At the trial, the patient presented evidence that the orderly had a history of drug and alcohol problems, that this was known to the hospital, that on one occasion the orderly was found drunk on the job, and that the hospital nevertheless allowed him to remain in the position until the molestation incident occurred.

In its defense, the hospital presented evidence that the orderly was a rehabilitated alcoholic who had had an exemplary employment record for the five years prior to the incident in question, that he began drinking again only a few months before the incident occurred, and that he was promptly terminated after the assault occurred. Nevertheless, on these facts, the jury found the hospital liable for nearly $200,000. 3/

These cases graphically show that, even though employers risk liability if they discipline employees too hastily for drug or alcohol problems, they also face potentially greater liability from injured third parties if they do not act swiftly and effectively to protect against harm caused by employees who are impaired by alcohol or drugs.

FOOTNOTES

CHAPTER 7

1. Horan v. Cold Spring Construction Co., 441 N.Y.S.2d 311 (1981).

2. Otis Engineering Corp. v. Clark, 668 S.W.2d 307 (1983).

3. Victoria v. Kaiser Foundation Hospitals, Case No. C-524-586, Los Angeles County Superior Court, reported in "Jury Verdicts Weekly," August 22, 1986. See also, Victoria v. Superior Court, 222 Cal.Rptr.1 (1985).

CHAPTER 8

CORPORATE STRATEGIES TO
CONTROL SUBSTANCE ABUSE

It is imperative that employers respond to the massive nationwide problem of substance abuse in the workplace, and that their responses be both effective and legally proper. The key elements of an appropriate response are discussed below.

Ascertaining The Facts

Employers must first educate themselves about the impact of the substance abuse problem in general, and how it may be affecting their own company in particular. Although it will not usually be possible to determine exactly how widespread the problem is within a particular workforce, a number of things can be done in an attempt to gauge the problem. In addition to documenting and reviewing any reports of drug dealing or drug and alcohol usage, employers should determine whether there has been an increase in security problems, such as employee theft or embezzlement, and review records of accidents, workers' compensation claims, injuries, quality control problems, productivity, absenteeism, or other indications of problems that might be attributable to substance abuse.

Corporate Commitment

Every employer must confront the problem of substance abuse directly and develop a comprehensive plan of attack. It is <u>not</u> advisable to ignore the problem and merely respond to individual incidents on an ad hoc basis.

While human resources staff can coordinate this effort, all other levels of management need to be committed to the project. It is critical that the CEO and other members of senior management have a keen understanding of the problem and be strongly committed to this effort if others in management, and throughout the company, are to support it.

Developing A Policy

It is important that a comprehensive policy be developed that addresses all aspects of the problem. The policy should be embodied in writing. It should set forth in general terms the company's overall philosophy and approach toward drugs and alcohol, as well as the specific rules and procedures that will be followed. Each employer's approach should be tailored to fit its circumstances, its corporate culture, its size, type of industry, the nature and composition of its workforce, and the severity of the substance abuse problem that is perceived to exist.

The statement of policy should contain rules clearly setting forth the types of conduct prohibited and the penalties for violation. Each employer must also decide what kinds of investigative or enforcement techniques it wishes to employ, including such methods as drug testing, searches, and undercover surveillance. If an employer wishes to reserve the right to administer drug or alcohol tests or to conduct searches of employees' lockers, desks or handbags, the written policy should clearly advise employees of these facts and set forth the ground rules. Employers should become familiar with the applicable privacy laws and ensure that their policies and practices are in conformity with those laws.

Employers must also decide what they wish to do about employees who violate their drug and alcohol rules, test positively for drugs, or are otherwise identified as having an actual or potential drug or alcohol problem. In this regard, every employer must carefully explore the extent to which it wishes to — or is legally required to — attempt to rehabilitate or provide employee assistance for substance abusers. Such rehabilitation efforts can take a wide variety of forms, including a sophisticated in-house employee assistance program, a referral to outside resources, or mere changes in the company's group health insurance coverage for drug and alcohol rehabilitation.

Once a company's substance abuse policy has been formulated and committed to writing, it should be fully communicated to everyone in the company through memoranda, bulletin board postings, meetings, employee handbooks, personnel manuals or other appropriate communications devices.

Administering Discipline

Bearing in mind the strict standards of proof applied by arbitrators (and likely to be applied by courts), employers should thoroughly investigate suspected violations of their drug and alcohol rules before finalizing discipline. It is better practice to suspend an employee pending further investigation than to make a hasty judgment on incomplete information. Employers should be as certain of the facts as is reasonably possible under the circumstances.

The rules should be consistently enforced. Performance problems and suspicious or improper conduct should be well documented in writing. Principles of progressive discipline should ordinarily be followed, as with other performance problems or rule infractions.

An employee should never be terminated because he or she is an alcoholic or has become dependent on drugs, nor should this be <u>stated</u> as the reason. Rather, discipline should be based on performance reasons (even if the poor performance is attributable to substance abuse) or the violation of clear company rules or policies. All employees should be held to the same performance, productivity, and attendance standards.

Employees manifesting a dependency on alcohol or drugs ordinarily should be given a firm choice between rehabilitation and discipline. They should be given clear, unequivocal, and uncompromising notice of possible discharge if their conduct does not change. Experts seem to agree that alcoholics and drug dependents will often go to extraordinary lengths to deny the existence of a problem. Thus, without the threat of imminent discharge, such persons may not be impelled to face up to the seriousness of the problem and the urgent need to correct it. Indecisive handling of such situations, or benign toleration of conduct that does not conform to the employer's standards, will not serve the best interests of the employer or the employee.

Sensitivity To Employees' Rights Of Privacy And Dignity

Employers should be continually mindful of the need to respect employees' legitimate rights and expectations of privacy and confidentiality in all matters relating to drugs and alcohol. An employee's participation in an employee assistance program or other form of rehabilitation should be kept confidential.

Medical records relating to any such treatment should never be disclosed to third persons without the employee's written authorization.

Investigations, searches, and the administration of chemical tests should be handled in as confidential and dignified a manner as possible under the circumstances, and should be conducted away from the presence of other employees. When an employee is disciplined for conduct related to drug or alcohol use, information about the reasons for the discipline should not be divulged to prospective employers or others — even to the employee's co-workers.

Training Supervisors

All managers and supervisors, especially first-line supervisors, should be knowledgeable about the company's rules and policies pertaining to drugs and alcohol, and its benefit programs. They should be fully trained in how to implement the policies and enforce the rules. They should become familiar with the most common symptoms of drug use, and should be trained in how to constructively confront employees who may need assistance for a drug or alcohol problem.

Supervisors should not attempt to diagnose the underlying causes of a performance dropoff, but should be able to spot the problem at an early stage and know how to properly respond to it. Finally, supervisors should be familiarized with the applicable laws, regulations and court doctrines pertaining to wrongful discharge, defamation, handicap-discrimination and privacy, so they will know how to avoid the legal pitfalls.

Employee Education

The company's substance abuse policy, as well as the reasons for it and the considerations that went into it, should be fully explained to all employees. This should include an explanation of the company's employee assistance or benefit programs, as well as its disciplinary policies and the consequences of engaging in violative conduct. Employees' cooperation and input should be solicited. This educational process should be a continuing one.

Relations With The Union

Employers should survey their existing collective bargaining contracts to determine their rights in regard to matters of substance abuse. Strategies for negotiating needed changes in the contract should be devised. Employers need to be mindful of unionized employees' "Weingarten" right to have a union representative present during investigatory interviews of employees who are suspected of violating the rules.

Employers should pursue cooperative efforts with union representatives as much as possible. While employers may, in certain circumstances, have the right to implement work rules unilaterally, successful implementation of a substance abuse policy will be accomplished more smoothly with union support and involvement. Unions have a common institutional interest with employers in supporting a responsible policy on substance abuse.

Conclusion

The problem of drugs and alcohol in the workplace defies easy analysis or easy solutions. The practical and legal complexities are considerable.

Nevertheless, the problem requires and deserves a strong, vigilant and enlightened approach by all employers. Because workplace substance abuse is just beginning to receive close scrutiny, employers are urged to periodically re-examine their substance abuse policies to ensure that they remain in compliance with current legal requirements, that they employ current know-how, and that they are responsive to their companies' current needs.

APPENDIX

- Sample Substance Abuse Policy Statement

- Sample Employee Handbook Policies

- Checklist Of Substance Abuse Symptoms

- Excerpts From San Francisco Ordinance

- Proposed California Drug Testing Law
  (Senate Bill No. 2175)

- Proposed California Drug Testing Law
  (Assembly Bill No. 4242)

- McDonell v. Hunter Decision

- Shoemaker v. Handel Decision

SAMPLE SUBSTANCE ABUSE POLICY STATEMENT

XYZ Company has the responsibility to maintain a safe and efficient working environment. Employees who work while under the influence of drugs or alcohol present a safety hazard to themselves and their co-workers. Moreover, the presence of drugs and alcohol in the workplace limits our ability to produce high quality products. Accordingly, we are implementing procedures to ensure that XYZ Company continues to maintain its reputation as a quality employer.

1. The following conduct is grounds for discipline, up to and including termination:

   o Use, possession, sale, or solicitation of illegal drugs;

   o Unauthorized use of alcohol on Company premises;

   o Reporting to work under the influence of alcohol or illegal drugs.

   Employees with alcohol or drug dependencies are encouraged to seek assistance through Personnel.

2. The Company reserves the right to require employees, while on duty or on Company property (including parking lots), to agree to inspections of their persons, vehicles, lockers, and/or their personal property. If an employee withholds consent to such an inspection, the Company may discipline the employee, up to and including termination.

3. The Company reserves the right to investigate any possible violations of this Substance Abuse Policy. If an employee refuses to participate in such an investigation, which may include medical testing for alcohol or drug use, the Company may discipline the employee, up to and including termination.

* * *

We ask for your cooperation. We believe these procedures are necessary to ensure a safe and secure working environment for everyone at XYZ Company.

SAMPLE EMPLOYEE HANDBOOK POLICIES

No-Drug/Alcohol Rules

Employees are prohibited, while on duty or on Company property, from being under the influence of alcohol or non-prescription drugs. Moreover, employees may not possess, sell, solicit, or receive alcohol or non-prescription drugs while on duty or on Company property. Any employee who violates this policy shall be subject to discipline, up to and including termination.

* * *

Employees are prohibited from bringing onto Company premises, having possession of, being under the influence of, or consuming on Company premises or while on Company business, any intoxicant.

* * *

Employees are prohibited from bringing onto Company premises, having possession of, being under the influence of, or using, transferring, selling or attempting to sell on Company premises or while on Company business, any form of narcotic, depressant, stimulant or hallucinogen, excepting only the taking of a prescribed drug under the direction of a physician.

* * *

Use, possession, sale or solicitation of unauthorized drugs or alcohol on Company premises, or reporting to work intoxicated or under the influence of drugs is grounds for immediate termination. Employees with alcohol or drug dependencies are encouraged to seek assistance through Personnel.

* * *

88

Searches

Entry onto Company property is deemed consent to an inspection of person, vehicle, and/or personal property. If you do not consent to such inspections, please do not enter or remain on Company property. Company property includes Company parking lots.

* * *

This Facility contains very valuable equipment and merchandise. It is extremely important, in order to protect your job and the jobs of everyone employed here, that all employees pay close attention to the security of our Facility and all equipment and merchandise located in the Facility. Please notify your Supervisor immediately if you see anything suspicious, including the presence of strangers on the premises.

In order to ensure that materials are not being removed from our premises without authorization, and that no unauthorized materials are brought in, we must reserve the right to question and inspect or search any person on or leaving the premises, along with any packages or other items that person may be carrying. All lunch containers, briefcases, handbags, parcels, etc., are subject to inspection and search by Management at any time, as are employee locker areas. Please understand that these procedures are necessary for the safety and security of everyone at the Company, that they apply to anyone entering or leaving our premises, and that failure to submit to or cooperate in these procedures is grounds for disciplinary action up to and including immediate discharge.

* * *

The Company reserves the right to require employees while on duty or on Company property (including parking lots), to agree to inspections of their persons, vehicles, and/or their personal property. If an employee withholds consent to such an inspection, the Company has the right to discipline the employee, up to and including termination.

* * *

Testing

The Company reserves the right to require employees to undergo medical testing for alcohol and/or drug use. If an employee refuses to participate in such an investigation, the Company may discipline the employee, up to and including termination.

CHECKLIST OF SUBSTANCE ABUSE SYMPTOMS

- Inconsistent performance

- Frequent illnesses combined with impulsively taken sick days

- Moodiness

- Deterioration in personal grooming

- Bloodshot or dull eyes, dilated pupils

- Nervousness, trouble sitting still, talkativeness

- Unsteady gait, tremors

- Burns on hands

- Increased physical injuries, bruises

- Sleepiness

- Constant runny nose

- Euphoria, increased energy

- Impaired short-term memory

- Impaired logical thinking

- Slurred speech

- Poor muscle control

- Depression

- Detached attitude

EXCERPTS FROM THE SAN FRANCISCO ORDINANCE
PROHIBITING EMPLOYER DRUG TESTING OF EMPLOYEES

Sec. 3300A.5   EMPLOYER PROHIBITED FROM TESTING OF EMPLOYEES. No employer may demand, require, or request employees to submit to, to take or to undergo any blood, urine, or encephalographic test in the body as a condition of continued employment. Nothing herein shall prohibit an employer from requiring a specific employee to submit to blood or urine testing if:

(a)   the employer has reasonable grounds to believe that an employee's faculties are impaired on the job; and

(b)   the employee is in a position where such impairment presents a clear and present danger to the physical safety of the employee, another employee or to a member of the public; and

(c)   the employer provides the employee, at the employer's expense, the opportunity to have the sample tested or evaluated by State licensed independent laboratory/testing facility and provides the employee with a reasonable opportunity to rebut or explain the results.

In conducting those tests designed to identify the presence of chemical substances in the body, and not prohibited by this section, the employer shall ensure to the extent feasible that the test only measure and that its records only show or make use of information regarding chemical substances in the body which are likely to affect the ability of the employee to perform safely his or her duties while on the job.

Under no circumstances may employers request, require or conduct random or company-wide blood, urine or encephalographic testing.

In any action brought under this Article alleging that the employer had violated this section, the employer shall have the burden of proving that the requirements of Subsections (a), (b) and (c) as stated above have been satisfied.

Sec. 3300A.6   MEDICAL SCREENING FOR EXPOSURE TO TOXIC SUBSTANCES.   Nothing in this Article shall prevent any employer from conducting medical screening, with the express written consent of the employees, to monitor exposure to toxic or other unhealthy substances in the workplace or in the performance of their job responsibilities. Any such screenings or tests must be limited to the specific substances expressly identified in the employee consent form.

Sec. 3300A.7   PROHIBITING USE OF INTOXICATING SUBSTANCES DURING WORKING HOURS; DISCIPLINE FOR BEING UNDER THE INFLUENCE OF INTOXICATING SUBSTANCES DURING WORKING HOURS. Nothing in this Article shall restrict an employer's ability to prohibit the use of intoxicating substances during work hours, or restrict an employer's ability to discipline employees for being under the influence of intoxicating substances during work hours.

AMENDED IN SENATE APRIL 1, 1986

SENATE BILL   No. 2175

Introduced by Senator Seymour

February 20, 1986

An act to add ~~Section 132.1 to~~ Article 3.5 (commencing with Section 440) to Chapter 3 of Part 1 of Division 2 of, to amend the heading of Chapter 3.7 (commencing with Section 1025) of Part 3 of Division 2 of, and to amend Sections 1025, 1026, and 1027 of, the Labor Code, relating to employment.

LEGISLATIVE COUNSEL'S DIGEST

SB 2175, as amended, Seymour. Employment: drug or alcohol testing.

Existing law does not prohibit an employer from testing employees for drug or alcohol use.

This bill would provide that an employer may require an employee ~~or applicant for employment to submit to or take any medical test to detect the presence of drugs or alcohol as a condition of employment only under unspecified circumstances.~~, as a condition of employment, to submit to or undergo a blood, urine, breath, or other chemical test to determine the presence in the body of alcohol or controlled substances, in specified circumstances, would require employers who conduct testing to take reasonable precautions to ensure the confidentiality of the test results, and would state the intent of the Legislature to occupy the field of regulation of substance abuse testing in employment to the exclusion of all local regulation.

This bill would specify that nothing in the bill would prohibit an employer from requiring an applicant for employment to undergo a blood, urine, or other chemical test to determine the presence in the body of alcohol or controlled substances.

Existing law requires a private employer regularly employing 25 or more employees to reasonably accommodate any employee who wishes to voluntarily enter and participate in an alcoholic rehabilitation program, provided that the reasonable accommodation does not impose an undue hardship on the employer.

This bill would also require a private employer regularly employing 25 or more employees to reasonably accommodate any employee who wishes to voluntarily enter and participate in a drug abuse rehabilitation program, provided that the reasonable accommodation does not impose an undue hardship on the employer.

Vote: majority. Appropriation: no. Fiscal committee: yes. State-mandated local program: no.

The people of the State of California do enact as follows:

1　SECTION 1. Section 432.1 is added to the Labor
2　Code, to read:
3　432.1. An employer may require an employee or
4　applicant for employment to submit to or take any
5　medical test to detect the presence of drugs or alcohol as
6　a condition of employment only under the circumstances
7　specified in this section.
8　SECTION 1. *Article 3.5 (commencing with Section*
9　*440) is added to Chapter 3 of Part 1 of Division 2 of the*
10　*Labor Code to read:*
11
12　*Article 3.5. Drug and Alcohol Testing*
13
14　*440. An employer may request or require an*
15　*employee, as a condition of continued employment, to*
16　*submit to or undergo a blood, urine, breath, or other*
17　*chemical test to determine the presence in the body of*
18　*alcohol or controlled substances, in any of the following*
19　*circumstances:*
20　*(a) Whenever the employer has a reasonable*
21　*suspicion that an employee or group of employees is, or*
22　*may be, impaired or affected on the job by alcohol or*
23　*controlled substances.*

1   *(b) Whenever the employer has a reasonable*
2   *suspicion that alcohol or controlled substances are*
3   *present in an employee's bodily system in violation of the*
4   *employer's published rules or policy.*
5   *(c) Whenever an employee has been involved in a*
6   *work-related accident causing bodily injury or damage to*
7   *property. however minor.*
8   *(d) As part of a physical examination which the*
9   *employer, under its established policies. requires*
10   *employees to undergo on a regular or periodic basis, or*
11   *as a result of specified occurrences. such as declining*
12   *performance or absenteeism, so long as employees are*
13   *notified in advance that the examination will include*
14   *testing for alcohol or controlled substances.*
15   *(e) In accordance with the terms of a collective*
16   *bargaining agreement between the employer and the*
17   *bargaining representative of its employees. or a written*
18   *employment agreement between an employer and an*
19   *employee.*
20   *(f) As part of the employer's program of rehabilitation*
21   *or employee assistance.*
22   *(g) Whenever an employee has tested positively for*
23   *the presence of alcohol or illegal controlled substances*
24   *within the prior 12-month period.*
25   *(h) As may be required or authorized by any federal*
26   *or state health, safety, or other law or regulation*
27   *441. In addition to the circumstances specified in*
28   *Section 440, an employer may conduct testing of*
29   *employees, including random, on-the-spot, or*
30   *company-wide testing, in any of the following*
31   *circumstances:*
32   *(a) Once in any 12-month period, regardless of the*
33   *employees' job classification.*
34   *(b) Up to three times in any 12-month period in the*
35   *case of employees whose jobs involve the operation of*
36   *vehicles in public transit, the operation of heavy*
37   *construction or off-shore oil drilling equipment, the*
38   *handling of hazardous substances, or any job in which*
39   *impairment due to alcohol or controlled substances*
40   *would present a safety hazard to employees or members*

1 of the public. However, before the testing of an
2 employee may be conducted pursuant to this section, the
3 employer shall advise the employee, in advance, of its
4 policy that the testing may be required.
5   442. Nothing in this article shall prohibit an employer,
6 or an agent thereof, from requiring an applicant for
7 employment to undergo a blood, urine, or other chemical
8 test to determine the presence in the body of alcohol or
9 controlled substances.
10   443. Employers who conduct testing pursuant to this
11 article shall take reasonable precautions to ensure the
12 confidentiality of the test results. Employers shall also
13 ensure that the substance abuse testing is not used for any
14 other purpose, such as testing for pregnancy, presence of
15 AIDS antibodies, or other medical or bodily conditions.
16   444. It is the Legislature's intention to occupy the
17 field of regulation of substance abuse testing in
18 employment encompassed by this article, exclusive of all
19 other laws regulating that testing in employment by any
20 city, county, city and county, or other political
21 subdivisions of this state. This article shall preempt and
22 take precedence over any local ordinance, law, or
23 regulation in the event of any conflict between that local
24 provision and this article.
25   SEC 2. The heading of Chapter 3.7 (commencing with
26 Section 1025) of Part 3 of Division 2 of the Labor Code is
27 amended to read:
28
29   CHAPTER 3.7. ALCOHOLIC OR DRUG ABUSE
30   REHABILITATION
31
32   SEC. 3. Section 1025 of the Labor Code is amended to
33 read:
34   1025. Every private employer regularly employing 25
35 or more employees shall reasonably accommodate any
36 employee who wishes to voluntarily enter and participate
37 in an alcoholic or drug abuse rehabilitation program,
38 provided that this reasonable accommodation does not
39 impose an undue hardship on the employer.
40   Nothing in this chapter shall be construed to prohibit

1 an employer from refusing to hire, or discharging an
2 employee who, because of the employee's current use of
3 alcohol *or drugs*, is unable to perform his or her duties, or
4 cannot perform the duties in a manner which would not
5 endanger his or her health or safety or the health or safety
6 of others.
7   *SEC. 4.   Section 1026 of the Labor Code is amended to*
8 *read:*
9   1026.   The employer shall make reasonable efforts to
10 safeguard the privacy of the employee as to the fact that
11 he or she has enrolled in an alcoholic *or drug abuse*
12 rehabilitation program.
13   *SEC. 5.   Section 1027 of the Labor Code is amended to*
14 *read:*
15   1027.   Nothing in this chapter shall be construed to
16 require an employer to provide time off with pay, except
17 that an employee may use sick leave to which he or she
18 is entitled for the purpose of entering and participating
19 in an alcoholic *or drug abuse* rehabilitation program.

AMENDED IN SENATE JUNE 24, 1986

AMENDED IN SENATE JUNE 12, 1986

AMENDED IN ASSEMBLY JUNE 9, 1986

AMENDED IN ASSEMBLY APRIL 23, 1986

AMENDED IN ASSEMBLY APRIL 2, 1986

CALIFORNIA LEGISLATURE—1985–86 REGULAR SESSION

ASSEMBLY BILL   No. 4242

Introduced by Assembly Members Klehs and Hauser
(Coauthors: Senators Roberti and Seymour)

February 21, 1986

An act to amend Section 1300 of the Business and Professions Code, to add Chapter 5 (commencing with Section 11998) to Part 5 of Division 10.5 of the Health and Safety Code, and to amend Sections 1025, 1026, and 1027 of, and to amend the heading of Chapter 3.7 (commencing with Section 1025) of Part 3 of Division 2 of, the Labor Code, relating to substance abuse.

LEGISLATIVE COUNSEL'S DIGEST

AB 4242, as amended, Klehs.   Alcohol and drug abuse.

(1) Under existing law, various fees are charged for applications and licensing of laboratories and laboratory personnel.

This bill would provide that the application fee for a clinical laboratory license is increased from $248 to $342 *$400* and the renewal fee from $196 to $292 *$355*, effective July 1, 1986 *January 1, 1987*.

(2) Under existing law, various provisions relate to alcohol and drug abuse.

This bill would enact the Substance Abuse Testing Act of

1986 to require that all employers requiring the testing of employees, both public and private, use specified licensed or certified laboratories. As applied to employers which are entities of local government, this would constitute a state-mandated local program.

(3) Under existing law, private employers regularly employing 25 or more employees are required to reasonably accommodate any employee who wishes to voluntarily enter and participate in an alcohol rehabilitation program, if this does not impose an undue hardship on the employer.

This bill would impose this requirement on public and private employers with respect to alcohol and drug rehabilitation programs. Public employers would be required to provide for alcohol and drug rehabilitation in conformity with these requirements and this would constitute a state-mandated local program.

(4) The California Constitution requires the state to reimburse local agencies and school districts for certain costs mandated by the state. Statutory provisions establish procedures for making that reimbursement, including the creation of a State Mandates Claims Fund to pay the costs of mandates which do not exceed $500,000 statewide and other procedures for claims whose statewide costs exceed $500,000.

This bill would provide that no reimbursement is required because the bill does not mandate a new program or higher level of service. It would recognize, however, that a local agency or school district may pursue reimbursement for any costs mandated by the bill pursuant to those statutory procedures.

Vote: majority. Appropriation: no. Fiscal committee: yes. State-mandated local program: yes.

The people of the State of California do enact as follows:

1   SECTION 1. Section 1300 of the Business and
2 Professions Code is amended to read:
3   1300. The amount of application and license fee
4 under this chapter shall be as follows:
5   (a) The application fee for a histocompatibility
6 laboratory director's, clinical laboratory bioanalyst's,

1 clinical chemist's, clinical microbiologist's, or clinical
2 laboratory toxicologist's license is thirty-eight dollars
3 ($38). This fee shall be sixty-three dollars ($63)
4 commencing on July 1, 1983.
5   (b) The annual renewal fee for a histocompatibility
6 laboratory director's, clinical laboratory bioanalyst's,
7 clinical chemist's, clinical microbiologist's, or clinical
8 laboratory toxicologist's license is thirty-eight dollars
9 ($38). This fee shall be sixty-three dollars ($63)
10 commencing on July 1, 1983.
11   (c) The application fee for a clinical laboratory
12 technologist's or limited technologist's license is
13 twenty-three dollars ($23). This fee shall be thirty-eight
14 dollars ($38) commencing on July 1, 1983.
15   (d) The annual renewal fee for a clinical laboratory
16 technologist's or limited technologist's license is fifteen
17 dollars ($15). This fee shall be twenty-five dollars ($25)
18 commencing on July 1, 1983.
19   (e) The application fee for a clinical laboratory license
20 is ~~three hundred forty/two dollars ($342) commencing on~~
21 ~~July 1, 1986~~ *four hundred dollars ($400) commencing on*
22 *January 1, 1987.* However, when the applicant is the state
23 or any agency or official thereof, or a district, city, county
24 or city and county, or an official thereof, no fee shall be
25 required.
26   (f) The annual renewal fee for a clinical laboratory
27 license is ~~two hundred ninety/two dollars ($292)~~
28 ~~commencing on July 1, 1986~~ *three hundred fifty-five*
29 *dollars ($355) commencing on January 1, 1987.* However,
30 when the applicant is the state or any agency or official
31 thereof, or a district, city, county, or city and county, or
32 official thereof, no fee shall be required.
33   (g) The application fee for a trainee's license is eight
34 dollars ($8). This fee shall be thirteen dollars ($13)
35 commencing on July 1, 1983.
36   (h) The annual renewal fee for a trainee's license is
37 five dollars ($5). This fee shall be eight dollars ($8)
38 commencing on July 1, 1983.
39   (i) The application fee for a duplicate license is three
40 dollars ($3). This fee shall be five dollars ($5)

AB 4242 —4—

1 commencing on July 1, 1983.
2   (j) The delinquency fee is equal to the annual renewal
3 fee.
4   (k) The director may establish a fee for examinations
5 required under this chapter. The fee shall not exceed the
6 total cost to the department in conducting the
7 examination.
8   SEC. 2. Chapter 5 (commencing with Section 11998)
9 is added to Part 5 of Division 10.5 of the Health and Safety
10 Code, to read:
11
12   CHAPTER 5. SUBSTANCE ABUSE TESTING
13
14   11998. This chapter shall be known and may be cited
15 as the "Substance Abuse Testing Act of 1986."
16   11998.1. The Legislature finds and declares all of the
17 following:
18   (a) Employers are increasingly using substance abuse
19 testing to screen job applicants and employees.
20   (b) The Centers for Disease Control report finds that
21 some of these tests may not be conducted properly. In a
22 1985 study, the CDC found "serious shortcomings" in the
23 quality controls of testing laboratories.
24   (c) Licensure of the state's laboratories which test on
25 behalf of employers will balance the rights of employees
26 with adequate protections for the public. Reducing illicit
27 drug use in the workplace will improve the safety, health,
28 and productivity of all Californians.
29   11998.2. If an employer requests or requires a job
30 applicant or an employee to submit to a substance abuse
31 test of any type, the employer shall use a clinical
32 laboratory licensed by the State Department of Health
33 Services under Chapter 3 (commencing with Section
34 1200) of Division 2 of the Business and Professions Code
35 or a public health laboratory certified by the state
36 department under Chapter 7 (commencing with Section
37 1000) of Division 1.
38   11998.3. Notwithstanding any negotiated collective
39 bargaining agreement between an employer and his or
40 her employees which provides for additional substance

1 abuse testing standards, employers shall inform
2 employees and job applicants of the testing policies in
3 writing upon the adoption of the policy or when the
4 employee is hired, if the policy was previously adopted.
5 An employee shall have the right to request a copy of the
6 results of a substance abuse test conducted pursuant to
7 this chapter.
8   11998.4.   Employers, employees, and laboratories shall
9 keep all samples and test results confidential in
10 compliance with the Information Practices Act of 1977
11 provided for in Chapter 1 (commencing with Section
12 1798) of Title 1.8 of Part 4 of the Civil Code and the
13 California Public Records Act provided for in Chapter 3.5
14 (commencing with Section 6250) of Division 7 of Title 1
15 of the Government Code.
16   11998.5.   This chapter shall apply to private employers
17 and to state and local entities of government.
18   SEC. 3.   The heading of Chapter 3.7 (commencing
19 with Section 1025) of Part 3 of Division 2 of the Labor
20 Code is amended to read:
21
22 CHAPTER 3.7. ALCOHOL AND DRUG REHABILITATION
23
24   SEC. 4.   Section 1025 of the Labor Code is amended to
25 read:
26   1025.   Every public and private employer regularly
27 employing 25 or more employees shall reasonably
28 accommodate any employee who wishes to voluntarily
29 enter and participate in an alcohol or drug rehabilitation
30 program, provided that this reasonable accommodation
31 does not impose an undue hardship on the employer.
32   Nothing in this chapter shall be construed to prohibit
33 an employer from refusing to hire, or discharging an
34 employee who, because of the employee's current use of
35 alcohol or drugs, is unable to perform his or her duties, or
36 cannot perform the duties in a manner which would not
37 endanger his or her health or safety or the health or safety
38 of others.
39   SEC. 5.   Section 1026 of the Labor Code is amended to
40 read:

AB 4242   — 6 —

1   1026. The employer shall make reasonable efforts to
2 safeguard the privacy of the employee as to the fact that
3 he or she has enrolled in an alcohol or drug rehabilitation
4 program.
5   SEC. 6. Section 1027 of the Labor Code is amended to
6 read:
7   1027. Nothing in this chapter shall be construed to
8 require an employer to do either of the following:
9   (a) Provide time off with pay, except that an
10 employee may use sick leave to which he or she is entitled
11 for the purpose of entering and participating in an
12 alcohol or drug rehabilitation program.
13   (b) Pay for the cost of an alcohol or drug rehabilitation
14 program.
15   SEC. 7. No reimbursement is required by this act
16 pursuant to Section 6 of Article XIII B of the California
17 Constitution because this act does not mandate a new
18 program or higher level of service on local government.
19 It is recognized, however, that a local agency or school
20 district may pursue any remedies to obtain
21 reimbursement available to it under Chapter 4
22 (commencing with Section 17550) of Part 7 of Division 2
23 of Title 2 of the Government Code.

Alan F. McDONELL, et al., Plaintiffs,

v.

Susan HUNTER, et al., Defendants.

Civ. No. 84–71–B.

United States District Court,
S.D. Iowa, C.D.

July 9, 1985.

Department of Corrections employees
brought action challenging constitutionality
of Department policy subjecting employees
to searches of vehicles and persons, seeking declaratory and injunctive relief. The
District Court, Vietor, Chief Judge, held
that: (1) strip search of correctional facility
employee may constitutionally be made
only on basis of reasonable suspicion,
based on specific objective facts and rational inferences that may be drawn from
those facts in light of experience; (2) it is
unreasonable to search employees' automobile parked outside confines within which
inmates are kept, even if parking lot is on
ground owned by correctional facility; (3)
Fourth Amendment allows Department of
Corrections to demand of an employee a
urine, blood or breath specimen for chemical analysis only on basis of reasonable
suspicion, based on specific objective facts
and reasonable inferences drawn from
those facts in light of experience, that employee is then under influence of alcoholic
beverages or controlled substances; and (4)
demand that employee submit urine specimen for chemical testing did not have reasonable suspicion basis, and was a demand
for a seizure not permissible under the
Fourth Amendment.

Ordered accordingly.

1. Searches and Seizures ⬅7(1, 10)

The Fourth Amendment is intended to
protect privacy of individuals from invasion
by unreasonable searches of person and
those places and things where an individual
has reasonable expectation of privacy; only

McDONELL v. HUNTER
Cite as 612 F.Supp. 1122 (D.C.Iowa 1985)

unreasonable searches are prohibited. U.S. C.A. Const.Amend. 4.

2. Searches and Seizures ⬙7(1)

Everyone is protected from unreasonable searches by the Fourth Amendment all the time, not just when police suspect someone of criminal conduct. U.S.C.A. Const.Amend. 4.

3. Searches and Seizures ⬙7(10)

One's person and one's automobile are places where one has reasonable or legitimate expectations of privacy, and government intrusions into those areas are searches within meaning of Fourth Amendment. U.S.C.A. Const.Amend. 4.

4. Searches and Seizures ⬙7(10)

Although there are significant limits to Fourth Amendment rights in an automobile, automobile is not an area totally devoid of one's reasonable expectation of privacy and Fourth Amendment protection. U.S.C.A. Const.Amend. 4.

5. Searches and Seizures ⬙1

Taking blood from body is a search and seizure within meaning of the Fourth Amendment. U.S.C.A. Const.Amend. 4.

6. Searches and Seizures ⬙1, 7(25)

Individual has reasonable and legitimate expectation of privacy in personal information contained in body fluids, and thus, governmental taking of a urine specimen is a seizure within meaning of the Fourth Amendment. U.S.C.A. Const. Amend. 4.

7. Searches and Seizures ⬙7(10)

Intrusions authorized by Department of Corrections' policy, which subjects employees to searches of vehicles, urinalysis, and blood tests, upon request of Department officials were intrusions into areas in which employees normally had reasonable and legitimate expectation of privacy protected by the Fourth Amendment, thus presenting question as to whether such intrusions were nevertheless reasonable and not violative of the Fourth Amendment. U.S.C.A. Const.Amend. 4.

8. Searches and Seizures ⬙7(10, 14)

Correctional facility security considerations reduce scope of reasonable expectations of privacy that one normally holds and makes reasonable some intrusions which would not be reasonable outside of facility; however, security considerations do not cause prisoners, visitors, or prison employees to lose all their Fourth Amendment rights at prison gates. U.S.C.A. Const.Amend. 4.

9. Searches and Seizures ⬙7(10)

Department of Corrections can constitutionally conduct such regulatory searches of persons entering correctional facilities, including employees, as are reasonably necessary to serve security considerations, but searches must be guided by some appropriate standards, and must be no more intrusive than is reasonably necessary. U.S.C.A. Const.Amend. 4.

10. Searches and Seizures ⬙7(10)

Routine search of all persons, including employees, entering correctional institution sufficiently intrusive to discover any hidden weapons is reasonable; such search can be accomplished by a magnetometer or pat-down search by person of same sex and inspection of contents of packages, purses, handbags and pockets. U.S.C.A. Const. Amend. 4.

11. Searches and Seizures ⬙3.3(2)

Strip search of correctional facility employee may constitutionally be made only on basis of reasonable suspicion, based on specific objective facts and rational inferences that may be drawn from those facts in light of experience; inchoate, unspecified suspicions are insufficient. U.S.C.A. Const.Amend. 4.

12. Drugs and Narcotics ⬙184

Generalized suspicion of drug smuggling activity by correctional facility employee is insufficient to justify strip search of employee; there must be reasonable grounds, based on objective facts, to believe that at time of strip search employee is concealing drugs on his or her person.

13. Drugs and Narcotics ⇐184

Correctional facility employee's mere association with another individual suspected of drug dealing does not provide independent basis for strip search of employee.

14. Searches and Seizures ⇐3.3(2)

Although bare anonymous tip that completely lacks any indicia of reliability will not satisfy reasonable suspicion standard necessary for strip search of correctional institution employee, if information in anonymous tip is linked to other objective facts, standard may be satisfied.

15. Searches and Seizures ⇐3.3(3)

If a tip is not anonymous, identity of informant, his reliability, and detail of information supplied may establish reasonable suspicion necessary for strip search of correctional facility employee.

16. Searches and Seizures ⇐7(10)

Although search of all automobiles brought within confines of correctional facility where they may be reached by inmates is reasonable, it is unreasonable to search a correctional facility employee's automobile that is parked outside confines within which inmates are kept, even if parking lot is on ground owned by correctional facility, and such a search violates the Fourth Amendment. U.S.C.A. Const. Amend. 4.

17. Searches and Seizures ⇐3.3(8)

Constitutionality of a search cannot rest on its fruits.

18. Searches and Seizures ⇐7(10)

Possibility of discovering which correctional institution employees might be using drugs and therefore might be likely to smuggle drugs to prisoners is far too attenuated to make seizures of employees' body fluids, pursuant to required taking of blood and urine samples of employees, constitutionally reasonable. U.S.C.A. Const. Amend. 4.

19. Searches and Seizures ⇐7(10)

Fourth Amendment allows Department of Corrections to demand of an employee a urine, blood or breath specimen for chemi-

cal analysis only on basis of reasonable suspicion, based on specific objective facts and reasonable inferences drawn from those facts in light of experience, that employee is then under influence of alcoholic beverages or controlled substances. U.S. C.A. Const.Amend. 14.

20. Searches and Seizures ⇐7(10)

Fourth Amendment does not preclude taking body fluid specimen as part of preemployment physical examination or as part of any routine periodic physical examination that may be required of employees, nor does it prohibit taking a specimen of blood, urine or breath on periodic basis as condition of continued employment under a disciplinary disposition if such condition is reasonably related to underlying basis for disciplinary action and duration of condition is specified and is reasonable in length. U.S.C.A. Const.Amend. 4.

21. Searches and Seizures ⇐7(28)

Search conducted pursuant to voluntary consent does not violate Fourth Amendment. U.S.C.A. Const.Amend. 4.

22. Searches and Seizures ⇐7(28)

In class action brought by employees of Department of Corrections challenging policy dealing with employee searches, District Court could not rest its decision as to reasonableness of searches on assumption that employees who signed consents voluntarily consented in advance to any search made under the policy, absent any evidence concerning circumstances of signing from which court could determine voluntariness. U.S.C.A. Const.Amend. 4.

23. Searches and Seizures ⇐7(27)

Consent form signed by some Department of Corrections employees as condition of employment served to alert employees to fact that their Fourth Amendment rights were more limited inside correctional institution, but was not a valid consent to any search other than one that was, under circumstances, reasonable and, therefore, permissible under the Fourth Amendment. U.S.C.A. Const.Amend. 4.

24. Officers and Public Employees ⚖110

Public employees cannot be bound by unreasonable conditions of employment.

25. Searches and Seizures ⚖7(27)

Advance consent to future unreasonable searches is not a reasonable condition of employment, and public employees cannot be bound to such consent. U.S.C.A. Const.Amend. 4.

26. Searches and Seizures ⚖7(10)

Demand that Department of Corrections employees submit urine specimen for chemical testing did not have a reasonable suspicion basis, and therefore was a demand for a seizure not permissible under the Fourth Amendment. U.S.C.A. Const. Amend. 4.

27. Searches and Seizures ⚖3.3(1)

Pat-down search of Department of Corrections employees entering correctional institution may be conducted without cause, but must be done uniformly or by systematic random selection, and not by discriminatory or arbitrary selection of persons to be searched.

28. Searches and Seizures ⚖3.3(3)

Searches of motor vehicles of Department of Corrections employees within confines of institution where vehicles are accessible to inmates, other than uniformly or by systematic random selection, may be made only on basis of reasonable suspicion, based on specific objective facts and reasonable inferences drawn from those facts in light of experience, that there is weapon or drugs or other contraband in motor vehicle to be searched.

———

Mark W. Bennett, Staff Counsel, Iowa Civil Liberties Union, Des Moines, Iowa, for plaintiffs.

Gordon Allen, Sp. Asst. Atty. Gen., Mark Hunacek, John Parmeter, Asst. Attys. Gen., Des Moines, Iowa, for defendants.

MEMORANDUM OPINION, FINDINGS OF FACT, CONCLUSIONS OF LAW AND JUDGMENT

VIETOR, Chief Judge.

This is a 42 U.S.C. § 1983 class action brought by three correctional institution employees challenging the constitutionality of an Iowa Department of Corrections policy (hereafter "the Department's policy" or "the policy") which subjects the Department's correctional institution employees to searches of their vehicles and persons, including urinalysis and blood tests, upon the request of Department officials.

The court previously entered an order, pursuant to Fed.R.Civ.P. 23(c)(3), certifying the class consisting of all individuals employed by the Iowa Department of Corrections at its various institutions throughout the state of Iowa who are covered by the Department's policies which may subject employees to searches of their personal motor vehicles and their persons, including strip-searches, and which allows Department of Corrections officials to demand urine, blood or breath specimens for chemical analysis.

Plaintiffs seek declaratory and injunctive relief on behalf of themselves and the class they represent that the Department's policy (a copy of which is attached hereto as Appendix A) violates the Fourth Amendment to the United States Constitution and plaintiffs' constitutional right to privacy.[1] Plaintiff McDonell also seeks back pay for earnings lost during his period of discharge.

Jurisdiction and venue are predicated upon 28 U.S.C. § 1343(3). Venue is proper in this district pursuant to 28 U.S.C. § 1392(a).

A preliminary injunction was issued in February of 1984, from which appeal was taken. The preliminary injunction order was affirmed. *McDonell v. Hunter*, 746 F.2d 785 (8th Cir.1984).

1. Although the Department's policy as written does not expressly mention submission of blood, urine and breath samples, there is no dispute that the policy is considered to include submission of such samples.

On June 6, 1985, the parties reported to the court that they have no further evidence to offer and no further briefing to present, so the case is now submitted for final decision on the evidence and briefs received by the court in conjunction with the preliminary injunction matter.

FINDINGS OF FACT

Plaintiff McDonell was employed as a correctional officer at the Men's Reformatory at Anamosa (hereinafter "Anamosa") until he was discharged on January 19, 1984. Shortly after that he was reinstated but transferred to a different institution. He lost ten days pay. Plaintiffs Curran and Phipps, at all times material to this action, were and continue to be employed at the Iowa Correctional Institution for Women at Mitchellville (hereinafter "Mitchellville").

There are approximately 1750 correctional institution employees of the Iowa Department of Corrections who are within the certified class.

Defendant Hunter is the Superintendent and chief executive officer of Mitchellville. Defendant Sebek is the Security Director of Mitchellville, and is responsible for the implementation and enforcement of the Department's policy. Defendant Behrends is the Acting Deputy Warden of Anamosa, and is responsible for the implementation of the Department's policy. Defendant Farrier is Director and chief administrative officer of the Iowa Department of Corrections, and is responsible for the supervision and operations of Anamosa, Mitchellville, and other correctional facilities.

It is, of course, necessary to maintain security at each correctional facility, and a necessary part of security is prevention of distribution of weapons, drugs and other contraband to inmates. The Department's policy challenged in this suit is designed to serve security requirements at the state's correctional facilities.

The motor vehicle parking lot for employees at Mitchellville is within the gates of the facility, that is, within the area where inmates are confined. At all other correctional facilities the employee parking lot is on facility property outside of the confines within which inmates are confined.

When plaintiff McDonell became employed at Anamosa in 1979, he signed a consent to search, a copy of which is attached hereto as Appendix B. On January 17, 1984, plaintiff McDonell was informed by supervisory personnel at Anamosa that they had received confidential information indicating that he had been seen the previous weekend with individuals who were "being looked at" by law enforcement officials regarding drug related activities. Based on this information, the supervisory personnel requested plaintiff McDonell to undergo urinalysis. He refused and as a result his employment was terminated on January 19. Shortly thereafter he was reinstated with loss of ten days pay and transferred to another institution.

In August of 1983, employees at Mitchellville were presented a search consent form to sign, a copy of which is attached hereto as Appendix C. Plaintiffs Curran and Phipps refused to sign. There is disputed evidence that they were initially told that they would not receive their paychecks if they did not sign. In any event, they did receive their paychecks and all paychecks since then, and they have not been discharged or disciplined in any way for refusing to sign.

The Department's policy does not identify who has the authority to require an employee to submit to a search or to provide a blood or urine sample, nor does the policy articulate any standards for its implementation. No separate written standards have been promulgated governing implementation of the Department's policy. In his affidavit, defendant Farrier states: "As a practical matter, correctional officers are not asked to submit to a urinalysis or blood test unless there is some articulable reason to believe that there may be a problem."

CONCLUSIONS OF LAW AND DISCUSSION

The Fourth Amendment to the United States Constitution states:

The right of the people to be secure in their persons, houses, papers, and effects, against unreasonable searches and seizures, shall not be violated, and no Warrants shall issue, but upon probable cause, supported by Oath or affirmation, and particularly describing the place to be searched, and the persons or things to be seized.

The Fourth Amendment applies to the states through the Fourteenth Amendment. *Wolf v. Colorado*, 338 U.S. 25, 27–28, 69 S.Ct. 1359, 1361, 93 L.Ed. 1782 (1949).

[1] The Supreme Court has rejected the notion of "constitutionally protected areas" and has said: "The fourth amendment protects people, not places." *Katz v. United States*, 389 U.S. 347, 351, 88 S.Ct. 507, 511, 19 L.Ed.2d 576 (1967). The Fourth Amendment is intended to protect the privacy of individuals from invasion by unreasonable searches of the person and those places and things wherein the individual has a reasonable expectation of privacy. *Terry v. Ohio*, 392 U.S. 1, 9, 88 S.Ct. 1868, 1873, 20 L.Ed.2d 889 (1968). Only "unreasonable" searches are prohibited. *Carroll v. United States*, 267 U.S. 132, 147, 45 S.Ct. 280, 283, 69 L.Ed. 543 (1925).

[2] Defendants suggest that Fourth Amendment considerations are not involved in this case because any searches made pursuant to the Department's policy would not be for criminal investigation purposes.[2] That contention is without merit. "It is surely anomalous to say that the individual and his private property are fully protected by the Fourth Amendment only when the individual is suspected of criminal behavior." *Camara v. Municipal Court*, 387 U.S. 523, 530, 87 S.Ct. 1727, 1731, 18 L.Ed.2d 930 (1967). *See Wyman v. James*, 400 U.S. 309, 317, 91 S.Ct. 381, 385, 27

L.Ed.2d 408 (1971). All of us are protected by the Fourth Amendment all of the time, not just when police suspect us of criminal conduct.

[3–6] There is no question that one's person and one's automobile are places where one has a reasonable or legitimate expectation of privacy, and that government intrusions into those areas are searches.[3] Taking blood from the body is a search and seizure within the meaning of the Fourth Amendment. *Schmerber v. California*, 384 U.S. 757, 767, 86 S.Ct. 1826, 1834, 16 L.Ed.2d 908 (1966). Urine, unlike blood, is routinely discharged from the body, so no governmental intrusion into the body is required to seize urine. However, urine is discharged and disposed of under circumstances where the person certainly has a reasonable and legitimate expectation of privacy. One does not reasonably expect to discharge urine under circumstances making it available to others to collect and analyze in order to discover the personal physiological secrets it holds, except as part of a medical examination. It is significant that both blood and urine can be analyzed in a medical laboratory to discover numerous physiological facts about the person from whom it came, including but hardly limited to recent ingestion of alcohol or drugs. One clearly has a reasonable and legitimate expectation of privacy in such personal information contained in his body fluids. Therefore, governmental taking of a urine specimen is a seizure within the meaning of the Fourth Amendment. *Allen v. City of Marietta*, 601 F.Supp. 482, 488–89 (N.D.Ga.1985); *Storms v. Coughlin*, 600 F.Supp. 1214, 1217–18 (S.D.N.Y.1984); *Murray v. Haldeman*, 16 M.J. 74, 81 (C.M.A.1983).

United States v. Skipwith, 482 F.2d 1272, 1277–79 (5th Cir.1973).

3. There are significant limits to Fourth Amendment rights in an automobile. However, an automobile is not an area totally devoid of one's reasonable expectation of privacy and Fourth Amendment protection, as suggested by defendants.

---

2. It may well be that the primary purpose of a search made under the Department's policy would be to serve the facility's security needs. However, if the search yielded drugs or an illegal weapon or illegal possession of a lawful weapon, a criminal prosecution could follow and the evidence uncovered, if constitutionally obtained, could be used in the prosecution.

[7] It is this court's conclusion that all of the intrusions authorized by the Department's policy are intrusions into areas where plaintiffs and their class normally have a reasonable and legitimate expectation of privacy protected by the Fourth Amendment. The question then becomes whether the intrusions authorized by the policy are nevertheless reasonable and therefore not violative of the Fourth Amendment.

Whether the authorized intrusions are reasonable must be evaluated in the context of the places of employment—penal institutions where security is a paramount consideration. The United States Court of Appeals for the Eighth Circuit, in a case involving the constitutionality of strip searching a prison inmate's visitor, stated:

The penal environment is fraught with serious security dangers. Incidents in which inmates have obtained drugs, weapons, and other contraband are well-documented in case law and regularly receive the attention of the news media. Within prison walls, a central objective of prison administrators is to safeguard institutional security. To effectuate this goal prison officials are charged with the duty to intercept and exclude by all reasonable means all contraband smuggled into the facility. Indeed, Iowa correctional officials recognize their duty to constrict the flow of contraband into the prison. They consider both clothed and unclothed body searches an effective means of controlling contraband and "a basic implement of the institutions['] overall security."

Although the preservation of security and order within the prison in unquestionably a weighty state interest, prison officials are not unlimited in ferreting out contraband. Certainly, as has been observed, one's anatomy is draped with constitutional protection. *United States*

v. *Afanador*, 567 F.2d 1325, 1331 (5th Cir.1978). And the state's interest must be balanced against the significant invasion of privacy occasioned by a strip search. Indeed, a strip search, regardless how professionally and courteously conducted, is an embarrassing and humiliating experience. *See United States v. Sandler*, 644 F.2d 1163, 1167 (5th Cir. en banc 1981); *United States v. Dorsey*, 641 F.2d 1213, 1217 (7th Cir.1981); *cf. Terry v. Ohio*, 392 U.S. at 24–25, 88 S.Ct. at 1881–1882 (limited search of outer clothing for weapons is likely to be an annoying, frightening, and perhaps humiliating experience).

Hunter v. Auger, 672 F.2d 668, 674 (8th Cir.1982).

[8] Correctional facility security considerations reduce the scope of reasonable expectations of privacy that one normally holds and makes reasonable some intrusions that would not be reasonable outside of the facility. However, security considerations do not cause prisoners to lose *all* of their constitutional rights at the prison gates. *Bell v. Wolfish*, 441 U.S. 520, 558–59, 99 S.Ct. 1861, 1884–85, 60 L.Ed.2d 447 (1979); *Wolff v. McDonnell*, 418 U.S. 539, 555–56, 94 S.Ct. 2963, 2974–75, 41 L.Ed.2d 935 (1974). Visitors do not lose *all* of their Fourth Amendment rights at the prison gates. *Hunter v. Auger, supra*. And prison employees do not lose *all* of their Fourth Amendment rights at the prison gates. *Armstrong v. New York State Commissioner of Correction*, 545 F.Supp. 728, 730 (N.D.N.Y.1982).

[9] There is no doubt that defendants can constitutionally conduct such "regulatory" searches of persons entering Iowa's correctional facilities, including employees, as are reasonably necessary to serve security considerations, but the searches must be guided by some appropriate standards,[4]

---

4. A fundamental problem with the Department's policy is that it lacks any standards whatsoever for its implementation. Who can authorize or make a search or a demand for a blood or urine sample? Without any standards, it appears that any institutional officer may authorize or make

a search or demand for blood or urine at his or her own unfettered discretion, and that the procedures followed will be another matter within the unfettered discretion of the officer implementing the Department's policy. The only

1

and must be no more intrusive than is reasonably necessary. *Hunter v. Auger, supra; McMorris v. Alioto,* 567 F.2d 897 (9th Cir.1978). The lack of any standards is noted in footnote 4. The court now turns to the questions of the reasonable necessity for the searches authorized by the Department's policy, the reasonableness of the extent of the intrusions authorized, and purported consents to the searches.

Searches of the Person

[10] A routine search of all persons, including employees, entering a correctional institution sufficiently intrusive to discover any hidden weapons is certainly reasonable. This can be accomplished by a magnetometer or a pat-down search by a person of the same sex and an inspection of the contents of packages, purses, handbags and pockets. A strip search is another matter. The "reasonable suspicion" standard for strip searching an inmate's visitor was established in *Hunter v. Auger, supra,* and the same standard has been held to apply to searches of prison employees. *Security & Law Enforcement Employees District Council 82 v. Carey,* 737 F.2d 187 (2d Cir.1984).

[11–13] This court concludes that a strip search of a correctional facility employee may constitutionally be made only on the basis of reasonable suspicion, based on specific objective facts and rational inferences that may be drawn from those facts in light of experience. *Hunter v. Auger, supra,* 672 F.2d at 674. Inchoate, unspecified suspicions are insufficient. *Id.* Furthermore, a generalized suspicion of drug smuggling activity is insufficient—there must be reasonable grounds, based on objective facts, to believe that at the

time of the strip search the employee is concealing drugs on his or her person. *Id.* at 675. Also, mere association with another individual suspected of drug dealing does not provide an independent basis for a strip search. *Id.*

[14, 15] Defendants argue that "mere suspicion" rather than "reasonable suspicion" should be the standard for permitting strip searches of employees. They contend that the reasonable suspicion standard established for strip searches of inmate visitors in *Hunter v. Auger, supra,* should not apply to employees because employees, unlike inmate visitors, cannot be limited to non-contact association with inmates. This position is arguable, but I do not find it persuasive. As the court observed in *Hunter:* "[T]he state's interest must be balanced against the significant invasion of privacy occasioned by a strip search. Indeed, a strip search, regardless how professionally and courteously conducted, is an embarrassing and humiliating experience." *Id.* at 674. The intrusion of a strip search is the most extreme intrusion of personal physical privacy that can be made. Concededly, the state's interest that is to be balanced against that extreme intrusion of privacy is a weighty interest. However, I believe that the state's interest will not be significantly impaired by the reasonable suspicion standard. The standard is not unreasonably burdensome.[5] If an employee is suspected of smuggling drugs into an institution, but the suspicion falls short of being a reasonable suspicion, surveillance and investigation would often either dispel the suspicion as unfounded or elevate it to the quality of reasonable suspicion. Furthermore, the state has means other than strip searches to discourage and guard against smuggling of contraband to in-

standard is that an after-the-fact written report be made to the institution's manager.

5. *Illinois v. Gates,* 462 U.S. 213, 103 S.Ct. 2317, 76 L.Ed.2d 527 (1983), and *Hunter v. Auger,* 672 F.2d 668 (8th Cir.1982), should provide guidance to defendants. Although a bare anonymous tip—one that completely lacks any indicia of reliability—will not satisfy the reasonable suspicion standard, if the information in the

anonymous tip is linked to other objective facts the reasonable suspicion standard may be satisfied. Indeed, depending on the totality of the circumstances, even "probable cause" may be established. Of course, if a tip is not anonymous, the identity of the informant, his reliability, and the detail of the information he supplies may establish reasonable suspicion.

112

mates by institution employees. For instance, the state can, and certainly should, carefully screen and investigate the backgrounds of employment applicants. Also, drug smuggling by employees could no doubt be substantially deterred by criminal prosecution of any who are found bringing drugs into an institution. Iowa Criminal Code § 719.8. Lastly, if on a particular day an employee is the object of only mere suspicion, he could be directed to leave for the day and thereby not be given the opportunity for any contact with inmates. A balancing of the state's interest against the significant invasion of privacy occasioned by a strip search supports the constitutionality of a reasonable suspicion standard for strip searches of institution employees, but does not support the constitutionality of a mere suspicion standard.

Searches of Automobiles

[16, 17] A search of all automobiles brought within the confines of the facility where they may be reached by inmates is reasonable. However, it is unreasonable to search an employee's automobile that is parked outside the confines within which inmates are kept, even if the parking lot is on ground owned by the correctional facility. Defendants argue that if a search of an employee's automobile yields drugs, that would show that the employee probably uses drugs and might, therefore, be likely to smuggle drugs to inmates. Perhaps, but that reasoning is far too attenuated to make such a search a constitutionally reasonable one. Furthermore, the constitutionality of a search cannot rest on its fruits. The institutional security need for searching employees' cars parked outside the confines of the institution has not been shown.

Blood and Urine Samples

[18] Defendants urge in support of taking blood and urine samples of employees

the same reasons urged for searching employees' cars parked outside the gates— identifying possible drug smugglers. So might searches of employees' homes and taps on their telephones. The possibility of discovering who might be using drugs and therefore might be more likely than others to smuggle drugs to prisoners is far too attenuated to make seizures of body fluids constitutionally reasonable. Defendants also argue that taking body fluids is reasonable because it is undesirable to have drug users employed at a correctional institution, even if they do not smuggle drugs to inmates. No doubt most employers consider it undesirable for employees to use drugs, and would like to be able to identify any who use drugs. Taking and testing body fluid specimens, as well as conducting searches and seizures of other kinds, would help the employer discover drug use and other useful information about employees. There is no doubt about it—searches and seizures can yield a wealth of information useful to the searcher. (That is why King George III's men so frequently searched the colonists.) That potential, however, does not make a governmental employer's search of an employee a constitutionally reasonable one.

[19, 20] It is this court's conclusion that the Fourth Amendment allows defendants to demand of an employee a urine, blood, or breath specimen for chemical analysis only on the basis of a reasonable suspicion, based on specific objective facts and reasonable inferences drawn from those facts in light of experience, that the employee is then under the influence of alcoholic beverages or controlled substances.[6] *See Division 241 Amalgamated Transit Union (AFL–CIO) v. Suscy*, 538 F.2d 1264, 1267 (7th Cir.1976). *But see Allen v. City of Marietta, supra*, 601 F.Supp. at 491.

6. The Fourth Amendment, however, does not preclude taking a body fluid specimen as part of a pre-employment physical examination or as part of any routine periodic physical examination that may be required of employees, nor does it prohibit taking a specimen of blood, urine, or breath on a periodic basis as a condition of continued employment under a disciplinary disposition if such a condition is reasonably related to the underlying basis for the disciplinary action and the duration of the condition is specified and is reasonable in length.

Consent

Defendants contend that plaintiff McDonell and other class members who signed a written consent (Appendixes B and C) have validly consented to searches under the Department's policy.

[21] A search conducted pursuant to a voluntary consent does not violate the Fourth Amendment. *Schneckloth v. Bustamonte*, 412 U.S. 218, 93 S.Ct. 2041, 36 L.Ed.2d 854 (1973). "We hold only that when the subject of a search is not in custody and the State attempts to justify a search on the basis of his consent, the Fourth and Fourteenth Amendments require that it demonstrate that the consent was in fact voluntarily given, and not the result of duress or coercion, express or implied. Voluntariness is a question of fact to be determined from all the circumstances * * *." *Id.* at 248–49, 93 S.Ct. at 2058–59.

[22] Plaintiff McDonell signed a consent form several years ago when he took employment at Anamosa. There is no evidence concerning the circumstances of that signing from which the court can determine voluntariness. Plaintiffs Curran and Phipps did not sign consents. There is no evidence concerning the circumstances of signing by class members who did sign. Under this record, the court cannot rest its decision on an assumption that plaintiff McDonell and class members who signed consents voluntarily consented in advance to any search made under the Department's policy.

[23–25] Furthermore, it is this court's conclusion that the consent form does not constitute a blanket waiver of all Fourth Amendment rights. Within a correctional institution everybody's Fourth Amendment rights are necessarily more limited than they are outside of the institution, but as discussed at page 7 of this memorandum opinion, Fourth Amendment rights are not totally lost. The consent form, which it appears plaintiff McDonell and others signed as a condition of employment when they became employed, served to alert employees to the fact that their Fourth Amendment rights are more limited inside the correctional institution, but the consent cannot be construed to be a valid consent to any search other than one that is, under the circumstances, reasonable and, therefore, permissible under the Fourth Amendment. Public employees cannot be bound by unreasonable conditions of employment. *Pickering v. Board of Education*, 391 U.S. 563, 568, 88 S.Ct. 1731, 1734, 20 L.Ed.2d 811 (1968). Advance consent to future *unreasonable* searches is not a reasonable condition of employment.

Defendants' reliance on *Wyman v. James, supra*, is misplaced. *Wyman* involved a state statutorily authorized home visit by a caseworker to the home of a recipient of Aid to Families with Dependent Children. The court, assuming without holding that such a home visit was a search, concluded that it was reasonable and therefore not violative of the Fourth Amendment. The numerous factors relied on in *Wyman* clearly distinguish it from the instant case.

[26] The January 1984 demand on plaintiff McDonell that he submit a urine specimen for chemical testing did not have a reasonable suspicion basis, and therefore it was a demand for a seizure not permissible under the Fourth Amendment.

JUDGMENT AND INJUNCTION ORDER

It is the declaratory judgment of the court that the Department's policy, Appendix A attached hereto, violates the Fourth Amendment rights of plaintiffs and the certified class insofar as it permits searches and seizures prohibited by the following injunction.

[27] Defendants and their officers, agents, servants and employees are hereby enjoined from conducting searches of the persons of plaintiffs and members of the certified class (employees) pursuant to the Department's policy, except as follows:

(1) Employees entering, or who have entered, a correctional institution may be

searched by use of a magnetometer or similar device, by a pat-down search by a person of the same sex, and by an examination of the contents of pockets, bags, purses, packages and other containers. Such a search may be conducted without cause, but must be done uniformly or by systematic random selection, and not by discriminatory or arbitrary selection of persons to be searched.

(2) Any strip search or any other body search that is more intrusive than the type allowed by subparagraph (1) above may be made only on the basis of a reasonable suspicion, based on specific objective facts and reasonable inferences drawn from those facts in light of experience, that the employee to be searched is then in possession of a weapon or drugs or other contraband. Such a search is to be made only on the express authority of the highest officer present in the institution, made by one of the same sex in a private setting, and the specific objective facts shall be disclosed to the employee before the search is conducted and shall be reduced to writing and preserved.

Defendants and their officers, agents, servants and employees are hereby further enjoined from demanding from plaintiffs and members of the certified class (employees), pursuant to the Department's policy, any urine, blood or breath specimen for chemical analysis, except that they are not enjoined from:

(1) Demanding of an employee who has entered a correctional institution a urine, blood, or breath specimen for chemical analysis on the basis of a reasonable suspicion, based on specific objective facts and reasonable inferences drawn from those facts in light of experience, that the employee is then under the influence of alcoholic beverages or controlled substances. Such a demand is to be made only on the express authority of the highest officer present in the institution, and the specific

objective facts shall be disclosed to the employee at the time the demand is made and shall be reduced to writing and preserved.

(2) Requiring an employee-applicant or an employee to provide blood and urine specimens as part of a pre-employment physical examination or as part of any routine periodic physical examination that may be required of employees.

(3) Requiring an employee to periodically submit a specimen of blood, urine or breath as a condition of continued employment under a disciplinary disposition if such a condition is reasonably related to the underlying basis for the disciplinary action and the duration of the condition is specified and is reasonable in length.

[28] Defendants and their officers, agents, servants and employees are hereby further enjoined from searching privately owned motor vehicles belonging to or used by plaintiffs and members of the certified class (employees) pursuant to the Department's policy, except that motor vehicles that are parked within the institution's confines where they are accessible to inmates[7] may be searched without cause, but such searches must be done uniformly or by systematic random selection, and not by discriminatory or arbitrary selection of employees whose motor vehicles are to be searched. Searches of employees' motor vehicles within the institution's confines where they are accessible to inmates, other than uniformly or by systematic random selection, may be made only on the basis of a reasonable suspicion, based on specific objective facts and reasonable inferences drawn from those facts in light of experience, that there is a weapon or drugs or other contraband in the motor vehicle to be searched. Such a "reasonable suspicion" search is to be made only on the express authority of the highest officer present in the institution, and the specific objective facts shall be disclosed to the employee

---

7. The term "within the institution's confines where they are accessible to inmates" means within confines within which the general inmate population is kept. The term does not

mean within some outer perimeter where low security risk inmates are sometimes allowed to go on work details.

whose motor vehicle is searched before the search is conducted and shall be reduced to writing and preserved.[8]

It is the further judgment of the court that plaintiff McDonell shall be paid the ten days' salary that he lost in conjunction with his temporary discharge.

APPENDIX A

INSTITUTIONS—PERSONNEL

SEARCHES OF EMPLOYEES AND AUTOMOBILES AND PERMISSION TO INSPECT EMPLOYEE LIVING QUARTERS

Policy

Any employee or vehicle entering the grounds of an adult institution or facility may be inspected at any time for security reasons. Employees must be advised in writing by the institutional manager that such inspections of the person or vehicle are a condition of coming onto the grounds of an adult institution or facility to work. A written report of such an inspection shall be made to the institutional manager.

If an employee refuses to cooperate in such an inspection, the institutional manager is to immediately be notified. He, in turn, will render a decision as to whether or not the employee refusing to be inspected is to be relieved of duty pending disposition of the matter.

All institutions and facilities having employees living on State property shall prepare forms—and have said form signed by all employees living on State-owned or leased property. (See Appendix)

APPENDIX B

STATE OF IOWA
DEPARTMENT OF SOCIAL SERVICES
BUREAU OF INSTITUTIONS
DIVISION OF ADULT CORRECTIONS

SEARCHES OF EMPLOYEES AND PERMISSION TO INSPECT EMPLOYEE LIVING QUARTERS

Any employee or vehicle entering the grounds of an adult institution or facility may be inspected at any time for security reasons. Employees must be advised in writing by the Institution Manager that such inspections of the person or vehicle are a condition of coming onto the grounds of an adult institution or facility to work. A written report of such an inspection shall be made to the Institution Manager.

If an employee refuses to cooperate in such an inspection, the Institution Manager is to immediately be notified. He, in turn, will render a decision as to whether or not the employee refusing to be inspected, is to be relieved of duty pending disposition of the matter.

All institutions and facilitites having employees living on state property shall prepare forms—a copy of which is attached—and have said form signed by all employees living on state owned or leased property.

Revised 2-22-77

I, /s/ Alan McDonell , have read and understand Section II-A-6 of the Bureau of Corrections Manual and realize that due to the nature of work, type of institution, and attitudes of some of the residents confined herein, a personal search of all persons coming into and going out of the Men's Reformatory is of benefit to the administration to curtail the movement of contraband in the institution.

8. None of the injunctive relief granted herein precludes any search and seizure authorized by a judicially issued search warrant, or a search and seizure without a warrant made on the basis of "probable cause" within the meaning of the Fourth Amendment if made under one of the established exceptions to the Fourth Amendment's warrant requirement, or a search made pursuant to a valid and voluntary consent given immediately before the search is conducted.

116

APPENDIX B—Continued

My signature on this page constitutes my permission to be searched at any time while on State property by a staff member of the same sex that I am, when the staff member is directed to do so by the Warden, person acting in that capacity, or his designated representative. I, also, agree to submit to a urinalysis or blood test when requested by the administration of the Reformatory. I further agree to cooperate and assist in any and all investigations of a security or possible criminal nature when requested to do so. I hereby affix my signature knowingly and voluntarily, absent of any duress or coercion.

/s/ Alan McDonell _____   3/2/79 _____
Signature   Date

/s/ D. Williams _____
Witnessed by

APPENDIX C

Department of Social Services
Des Moines

SEARCHES OF EMPLOYEES AND PERMISSION TO INSPECT
EMPLOYEE LIVING QUARTERS FORM

I, _____, have read and understand Section II–C–5 of the Divison of Adult Corrections Manual and realize that due to the nature of work, type of institution, and attitudes of some of the residents confined herein, a personal search of all persons coming into and going out of the institution is of benefit to the administration to curtail the movement of contraband in the institution.

My signature on this page constitutes my permission to be searched at any time while on State property by a staff member of the same sex that I am, when the staff member is directed to do so by the Warden, person acting in that capacity, or his designated representative. I, also, agree to submit to a urinalysis or blood test when requested by the administration of the institution. I further agree to cooperate and assist in any and all investigations of a security or possible criminal nature when requested to do so. I hereby affix my signature knowingly and voluntarily, absent of any duress or coercion.

_____   _____
Signature   Date

_____
Witnessed by

William SHOEMAKER, Angel Cordero,
Jr., William Herbert McCauley, Philip
Grove, and Vincent Bracciole, Appel-
lants,

v.

Hal HANDEL, Executive Director of the
New Jersey Racing Commission, Sam-
uel A. Boulmetis, Steward Representing
New Jersey Racing Commission, Joseph
F. Piarulli, Associate Steward, Carl H.
Hanford, Associate Steward, and Rich-
ard W. Lawrenson, Associate Steward.

No. 85–5655.

United States Court of Appeals,
Third Circuit.

Argued April 18, 1986.
Decided July 10, 1986.

Jockeys brought action challenging
New Jersey Racing Commission regulations permitting State Racing Steward to
direct any official, jockey, trainer or groom
to submit to breathalyzer and urine testing
to detect alcohol or drug consumption.
The United States District Court for the
District of New Jersey, Stanley S. Brot-
man, J., 619 F.Supp. 1089, upheld the regulations with the proviso that results of
breathalyzer tests be subjected to same
confidentiality procedures provided for
urine tests. Jockeys appealed. The Court
of Appeals, Gibbons, Circuit Judge, held
that: (1) administrative-search exception
applied to warrantless breath and urine
testing of employees in heavily regulated
horse racing industry; (2) daily selection by
lot of jockeys to be subjected to urine testing did not violate Fourth Amendment; and
(3) privacy contentions of jockeys were not
ripe for adjudication.

Affirmed.

1. Searches and Seizures ⊜24, 79

In general a warrant is required for a
search to be considered reasonable under
the Fourth Amendment; however, in closely regulated industries, exception to war-

rant requirement exists for searches of premises pursuant to an administrative inspection scheme. U.S.C.A. Const.Amend. 4.

2. Searches and Seizures ⊂⊃79

To justify warrantless administrative-search exception, there must be a strong state interest in conducting an unannounced search, and pervasive regulation must have reduced the justifiable privacy expectation of the subject of the search.

3. Searches and Seizures ⊂⊃79

Administrative-search exception applied to warrantless breath and urine testing by New Jersey Racing Commission of employees in heavily regulated horse racing industry, considering that New Jersey had a strong interest in assuring public of integrity of persons engaged in industry, and that regulation of the industry has reduced justifiable privacy expectations of persons engaged in it.

4. Searches and Seizures ⊂⊃78

Daily selection by lot of jockeys to be subjected to urine testing by the New Jersey Racing Commission did not violate the Fourth Amendment; declining to follow *Security and Law Enforcement Employees, Dist. Council 82 v. Carey*, 737 F.2d 187 (2d Cir.). U.S.C.A. Const.Amend. 4.

5. Constitutional Law ⊂⊃230.3(1)

New Jersey State Racing Commission regulations authorizing administration of breathalyzer and urine tests for alcohol and drug use by jockeys did not violate equal protection on ground that while all jockeys had to submit to daily breathalyzer tests, officials, trainers, and grooms were not subject to daily testing and that only jockeys were currently subjected to random selection for urine testing; while state's interest in appearance of integrity of the racing industry reached to all participants, it was greatest with respect to jockeys, and state could rationally take one step at a time. U.S.C.A. Const.Amend. 14.

6. Constitutional Law ⊂⊃46(1)

Contention that breathalyzer and urine testing of jockeys by New Jersey Racing Commission, which involved collection of medical information, violated their rights of privacy with respect to such information was not ripe for adjudication, considering proposed regulatory amendments concerning confidentiality which would satisfy privacy concerns of jockeys.

William L. Bowe (argued), Bowe & Rakinic, Woodbury, N.J., Edward A. Rudley, Philadelphia, Pa., for appellants.

Irwin I. Kimmelman, Atty. Gen. of N.J., James J. Ciancia, Asst. Atty. Gen., Steven Wallach (argued), Deputy Atty. Gen., Trenton, N.J., for appellees.

Before ADAMS, GIBBONS and WEIS, Circuit Judges.

OPINION OF THE COURT

GIBBONS, Circuit Judge:

Five well known jockeys appeal from an adverse decision in their action seeking declaratory and injunctive relief against officials of the New Jersey Racing Commission. The action challenges the constitutionality of regulations adopted by the Commission that permit the State Racing Steward to direct any official, jockey, trainer, or groom to submit to breathalyzer and urine testing to detect alcohol or drug consumption. The regulations provide for sanctions of varying severity, including lifetime suspension from racing for persons testing positive. The jockey plaintiffs contend that the regulations violate their rights under the fourth, fifth, ninth, and fourteenth amendments to the Constitution. After a trial the district court made findings of fact and conclusions of law in which all of the jockeys' challenges to the regulations were rejected. 619 F.Supp. 1089 (1985). We affirm.

I.

The New Jersey Racing Commission regulates horse racing in that state. Its statutory powers include "full power to prescribe rules, regulations and conditions under which all horse races shall be conducted." N.J.Stat.Ann. § 5:5–30 (West 1973). The racing industry involves parimutuel wagering, and the state receives a part of the revenue derived from such wagering. N.J.Stat.Ann. §§ 5:5–64, 5:5–64.1 (West Supp.1985).

All parimutuel employees and all horse owners, riders, agents, trainers, stewards, starters, timers, judges, grooms, drivers, and others, acting in any capacity in connection with the training of the horses or the actual running of the races in any such race meeting may be licensed by the commission, pursuant to such rules and regulations as the commission may adopt.

Id. § 5:5–33. Because the public wagers on the outcome of races, the Commission's regulations have focused upon the necessity for preserving both the fact and the appearance of integrity of the racing performances. Thus, for example, the Commission's regulations for many years have placed on the trainer of a horse the absolute duty, regardless of fault, to protect the horse from the administration of drugs that might affect its performance. *See Dare v. State ex rel. Department of Law and Public Safety, Division of New Jersey Racing Commission*, 159 N.J.Super. 533, 538–89, 388 A.2d 984, 986 (App.Div.1978)

(per curiam). Moreover to assure the discharge of this duty, the Commission's regulations have for many years provided for postrace specimen testing of horses and, if tests prove positive for a drug or foreign substance, for warrantless searches of the premises occupied by the stable involved. *See State v. Dolce*, 178 N.J.Super. 275, 284–87, 428 A.2d 947, 952–54 (App.Div. 1981). The present version of these regulations is in Subchapter 14A of the Commission's regulations, entitled Medication and Testing Procedures. N.J.Admin.Code tit. 13, §§ 70–14A.1 to 70–14A.11 (1985).

The regulations challenged in this action are also parts of Subchapter 14A. They were proposed by notice in the New Jersey Register in 1984 and adopted in January 1985, effective as of April 1, 1985. The first regulation requires that officials, jockeys, trainers, and grooms shall, when directed by the State Steward, submit to breathalyzer tests for the detection of alcohol.[1] The second regulation provides that every official, jockey, trainer, and groom for any race may be subjected to a urine test for the detection of use of "Controlled Dangerous Substance[s]", and may be subjected to sanctions for failure to submit to such a test, and for positive results in such a test.[2]

1. The regulation provides in full.

Officials, jockeys, trainers and grooms shall, when directed by the State Steward, submit to a breathalyzer test and if the results thereof show a reading of more than .05 percent of alcohol in the blood, such person shall not be permitted to continue his duties. The stewards may fine or suspend any participant who records a blood alcohol reading of .05 percent or more. Any participant who records a reading above the prescribed level on more than one occasion shall be subject to expulsion, or such penalty as the stewards may deem appropriate.

N.J.Admin.Code tit. 13, § 70–14A.10 (1985).

This regulation is similar to a regulation that has applied to harness race drivers since 1969. N.J.Admin.Code tit. 13, § 71–18.1 (1985).

2. This regulation provides in full.

(a) No licensee or official shall use any Controlled Dangerous Substance as defined in the "New Jersey Controlled Dangerous Substance Act", N.J.S.A. 24:21–1, et seq. or any prescription legend drug, unless such substance was obtained directly, or pursuant to a

valid prescription or order from a licensed physician, while acting in the course of his professional practice. It shall be the responsibility of the official, jockey, trainer and groom to give notice to the State Steward that he is using a Controlled Dangerous Substance or prescription legend drug pursuant to a valid prescription or order from a licensed practioner when requested.

(b) Every official, jockey, trainer and groom for any race at any licensed racetrack may be subjected to a urine test, or other non-invasive fluid test at the direction of the State Steward in a manner prescribed by the New Jersey Racing Commission. Any official, jockey, trainer or groom who fails to submit to a urine test when requested to do so by the State Steward shall be liable to the penalties provided in N.J.A.C. 13:70–31.

(c) Any official, jockey, trainer and groom who is requested to submit to a urine test shall provide the urine sample, without undue delay, to a chemical inspector of the Commission. The sample so taken shall be immediately sealed and tagged on the form provided

Shortly after the effective date of the regulations, the jockeys, all of whom are licensed by the Commission, filed this action pursuant to section 1983 of title 42 of the United States Code, 42 U.S.C. § 1983 (1982), seeking to restrain the Commission and its agents from enforcing the regulations on the grounds that the regulations were unconstitutional. The plaintiffs moved for a preliminary injunction, which the district court denied. The defendants moved for a dismissal of the complaint or for summary judgment, which the court also denied. After a bench trial the district court denied injunctive relief.

The district court's findings, which are not disputed, establish that jockeys are required to take a breathalyzer test daily, while grooms, trainers, and officials are tested less frequently. The breathalyzer apparatus is set up in or near the jockey's room and is run by an operator. The test, which requires that the jockey step up to a machine and breathe, is painless. The machine determines the level of blood alcohol from the expelled breath and indicates a positive reading by means of a red light visible to others in the room.

The district court found that while post-race urine tests are required "at the di-

by the Commission and the evidence of such sealing shall be indicated by the signature of the tested official, jockey, trainer or groom. The portion of the form which is provided to the laboratory for analysis shall not identify the individual official, jockey, trainer or groom by name. It shall be the obligation of the official, jockey, trainer or groom to cooperate fully with the Chemical Inspector in obtaining any sample which may be required to witness the securing of such sample.

(d) A "positive" Controlled Dangerous Substance or prescription drug result shall be reported, in writing, to the Executive Director or his designee. On receiving written notice from the official chemist that a specimen has been found "positive" for controlled dangerous substances or prescription legend drug, the Executive Director or his designee shall proceed as follows:

1. He shall, as quickly as possible, notify the official, jockey, trainer and groom involved in writing.

2. For an official, jockey, trainer or groom's first violation, he shall issue a written reprimand and warning and notify the official, jockey, trainer or groom that he will be subject to mandatory drug testing and that any further violation shall result in the sanctions described in paragraphs (3) and (4) below:

3. For an official, jockey, trainer or groom's second violation, he shall require the official, jockey, trainer or groom to enroll in a Supervisory Treatment Program approved by the New Jersey Racing Commission upon such reasonable terms and conditions as he may require. The official, jockey, trainer or groom shall be permitted to participate unless his continued participation shall be deemed, by the Executive Director or his designee, to be detrimental to the best interests of racing. It shall be the official, jockey, trainer or groom's responsibility to provide the Commission with written notice of his enrollment,

weekly status reports and written notice that he has successfully completed the program and has been discharged. If an official, jockey, trainer or groom fails to comply with these requirements, he shall be liable to the penalties provided in N.J.A.C. 13:70–31.

4. For official, jockey, trainer or groom's third or subsequent violation, he shall be liable to the penalties provided in Subchapter 31 and may only enroll into a Supervisory Treatment Program in lieu of said penalties, with the approval of the New Jersey Racing Commission.

(e) Any information received in the process of obtaining a urine sample, including but not limited to medical information, the results of any urine test, and any reports filed as a result of attending a Supervisory Treatment Program shall be treated as confidential, except for their use with respect to a ruling issued pursuant to this rule, or any administrative or judicial hearing with regard to such a ruling. Access to the information received and/or reports of any positive results and/or reports from a Supervisory Treatment Program shall be limited to the Commissioners of the New Jersey Racing Commission, the Executive Director and/or his designee, Counsel to the Racing Commission and the subject, except in the instance of a contested matter. In the instance of a contested matter, any information received and reports prepared shall not be disclosed without the approval of the Executive Director or his designee.

(f) Information received and reports prepared pursuant to this rule shall be stored in a locked secure area in the office of the Executive Director for a period of one year, after which time, they shall be destroyed. However, the Commission may maintain the information received and reports on individuals who have violated this rule for the purpose of recording the number of violations and the results of supervisory treatment, and for use should future violations occur.

N.J.Admin.Code tit. 13, § 70–14A.11 (1985).

rection of the State Steward," N.J.Admin. Code tit. 13, § 70–14A.11(b), the Commission has implemented the urine testing program by a method of random selection. The names of all participating jockeys at a given race are placed in an envelope. The State Steward or a representative draws the names of three to five jockeys for testing. A representative of the Jockey's Guild is invited to supervise the selection of names. The Commission may alter the number of names to be drawn each day. If a jockey's name is drawn more than three times in a seven-day period, the steward disregards the selection and draws another name. The jockeys whose names are selected must provide urine samples after their last race of the day. They are given plastic containers for this purpose. They are also required to fill out certification forms concerning the use of prescription or non-prescription medications. The certification form is to provide information about drugs covered by an exception in the regulations for any "substance ... obtained directly, or pursuant to a valid prescription or order from a licensed physician." N.J. Admin.Code tit. 13, § 70–14A.11(a). The form, as currently in use, provides for the optional disclosure of the condition for which the disclosed drug is a treatment. The certification forms contain two identical numbers. One number is removed and fastened to the urine sample, while the other number remains on the form. The anonymous urine sample is then sent to a laboratory for testing, and the form is sent to the Executive Director of the Commission and stored in a safe.

Urine test results are sent by the laboratory to the Executive Director and are available to that official, a designee, and the Commissioners. Pursuant to the express provisions of the regulations, the results are kept confidential even from the enforcement agencies. N.J.Admin.Code tit. 13, § 70–14A.11(e). The test results may only be used "with respect to a ruling issued pursuant to [section 70–14A.11], or any administrative or judicial hearing with regard to such a ruling." Id. The New Jersey Division of Criminal Justice, which

is headed by the Attorney General, has issued an advisory opinion voicing no objection to the confidentiality regulation and stating that it is unaware of any statute that would require the Commission to report suspected drug use to any prosecutorial authorities. On May 24, 1985, while this action was pending, the Commission proposed amendments to the urine-testing regulation to broaden the confidentiality requirements so as to cover all information obtained pursuant to the rule, to prohibit disclosure without approval of the Executive Director of the Commission or a designee and to destroy test results after a year except when violations have been discovered. N.J.Admin.Code tit. 13, § 70–14A.11(f) (1985). During the comment period before the proposed amendments to the rule became effective the Commission treated the collected information as if the confidentiality amendments were in effect.

The breathalyzer regulation does not provide for the preservation of confidentiality of results nor for privacy of administration. N.J.Admin.Code tit. 13, § 70–14A.10. The Commission prefers, however, to administer the breathalyzer tests in private.

Jockeys "reduce" or lose weight quickly, by eliminating excess body fluids so as to lighten the load a horse must carry in a race. This lessens their ability promptly to provide postrace urine samples. Thus many jockeys selected for urine sampling have been delayed after their last race for up to an hour. If the State Steward determines that a jockey cannot provide a sample, the jockey is excused and retested the next day. If the jockey leaves without giving a sample or without being excused, the State Steward will notify the jockey of a hearing, and the jockey may be subject to the penalties. See N.J.Admin.Code tit. 13, § 70–31.3 (1982). Those penalties include fines, suspensions, and loss of license. Id.

Positive test results in the urine test may disclose not only use of drugs at the race track, but also off-premises drug use for as long as a week prior to the day of the test. The prohibition in the Commission's regulations against use of controlled substances applies to any such use. N.J.Admin.Code tit. 13, § 70:14A.11(a).

II.

The jockeys do not contend that jockeys with more than .05 percent of alcohol in their blood should be permitted to ride. Thus they do not challenge the substantive prohibition in section 70–14A.10. Nor do they contend that they should be free to use controlled substances. Rather, they contend (1) that both regulations are unconstitutional facially and as applied in that they authorize searches and seizures that violate the fourth amendment; (2) that the enforcement scheme deprives them of equal protection of the laws; and (3) that the enforcement scheme violates their constitutional right to privacy.

A. The Fourth Amendment

The jockeys urge that neither the mandatory daily breathalyzer test nor the random urine test may be required without an individualized suspicion. The jockeys concede that if the racing officials are aware of specific objective facts suggesting that certain persons have recently used alcohol or drugs a warrantless production of a breath or urine sample could be demanded. Focusing particularly on section 70–14A.11(b), they contend that this regulation vests far too much discretion in the Commission as to who will be targeted for testing. The Commission does not argue that the mandatory tests do not involve a search or seizure within the meaning of the Fourth Amendment. Instead it urges that such warrantless searches or seizures by volun-

tary participants in the highly regulated racing industry are reasonable.

Since 1939, when article IV, section 7, paragraph 2 of the New Jersey Constitution was amended to make it lawful "to hold, carry on, and operate in this state race meetings whereat the trotting, running or steeplechase racing of horses ... may be conducted ... at which the pari-mutuel system of betting shall be permitted," [3] the horse racing industry has been among the state's most highly regulated industries. That constitutional provision was implemented into legislation that established the Commission and gave it broad rulemaking authority. *See* Pub.L. 1940 c. 17, §§ 1–58 (codified as amended at N.J. Stat.Ann. § 5:5–22 to 5:5–99 (West 1973 and West Supp.1985)). From its initial enactment, the statute permitted the licensing of all employees in the industry. Pub.L. 1940, c. 17, p. 74, § 13 (codified as amended at N.J.Stat.Ann. § 5:5–33 (West Supp. 1985)). Because of the state's interest in the revenue generated by wagering and the vulnerability of the industry to untoward influences, the statute has always provided that no person could be employed in any capacity at a racetrack "who has been convicted of a crime involving moral turpitude." Pub.L. 1940, c. 17, p. 75, § 14 (codified at N.J.Stat.Ann. § 5:5–34).[4] From the beginning the Commission has had the authority to prescribe conditions under which licenses may be issued and revoked. N.J.Stat.Ann. § 5:5–33. Thus all licensees have always participated in the industry with full awareness that it is the subject of intense state regulation. Those regulations have two separate but interrelated

---

3. *See* N.J. Const. 1844, art. IV, § 7, par. 2, as amended in 1939. The 1939 amendment is reprinted in *Revised Statutes of New Jersey Cumulative Supplement Laws of 1938 & 1939* XVI (J. Sarnoff ed. 1940). *See also Atlantic City Racing Ass'n v. Attorney General*, 98 N.J. 535, 541, 489 A.2d 165, 168 (1985) (reprinting the 1939 amendment). In 1947 New Jersey revised its 1844 Constitution. The current version of article iv, section 7, paragraph 2 does not contain any specific reference to pari-mutuel betting on horse racing. *See* N.J. Const. 1947, art. IV, § 7, par. 2, *reprinted as amended in* N.J.Stat.Ann. (West.Supp.1985). Instead the authority for bet-

ting on horse racing allowed by the 1939 amendment was incorporated by indirect reference in the first clause of article IV, section 7, paragraph 2 of the 1947 Constitution. *See* 1 & 2 *State of New Jersey Constitution Convention of 1947*, 355, 427–47, 1095.

4. The literal stricture of this provision probably is modified by the Rehabilitated Convicted Offenders Act, N.J.Stat.Ann. §§ 2A:168A–1 to 168A–6 (West 1985). *See Maietta v. New Jersey Racing Comm'n*, 183 N.J.Super. 397, 444 A.2d 55, 59–60 (App.Div.1982), *aff'd*, 93 N.J. 1, 459 A.2d 295 (1983).

purposes; the protection of the wagering public, and the protection of the state's fisc by virtue of the wagering public's confidence in the integrity of the industry.

[1] In general a warrant is required for a search to be considered reasonable under the fourth amendment. *See, e.g., Payton v. New York*, 445 U.S. 573, 586, 100 S.Ct. 1371, 1380, 63 L.Ed.2d 639 (1980); *See v. City of Seattle*, 387 U.S. 541, 545, 87 S.Ct. 1737, 1740, 18 L.Ed.2d 943 (1967). In closely regulated industries, however, an exception to the warrant requirement has been carved out for searches of premises pursuant to an administrative inspection sheme. *See, e.g., Donovan v. Dewey*, 452 U.S. 594, 602–05, 101 S.Ct. 2534, 2539–41, 69 L.Ed.2d 262 (1981) (coal mines); *United States v. Biswell*, 406 U.S. 311, 316–17, 92 S.Ct. 1593, 1596–97, 32 L.Ed.2d 87 (1972) (gun selling); *Colonnade Catering Corp. v. United States*, 397 U.S. 72, 76–77, 90 S.Ct. 774, 776–77, 25 L.Ed.2d 60 (1970) (liquor industry). Although it it clear that the New Jersey horse-racing industry is closely regulated, the question that arises in this case is whether the administrative search exception extends to the warrantless testing of persons engaged in the regulated activity.

[2] There are two interrelated requirements justifying the warrantless administrative search exception. First, there must be a strong state interest in conducting an unannounced search. *See Donovan*, 452 U.S. at 600, 100 S.Ct. at 1387. Second, the pervasive regulation of the industry must have reduced the justifiable privacy expectation of the subject of the search. *Id.* Both these requirements are present in the warrantless testing of persons involved in the New Jersey horse racing industry.

[3] New Jersey has a strong interest in assuring the public of the integrity of the persons engaged in the horse racing industry. Public confidence forms the foundation for the success of an industry based on wagering. Frequent alcohol and drug testing is an effective means of demonstrating that persons engaged in the horse racing industry are not subject to certain outside influences. It is the public's perception, not the known suspicion, that triggers the state's strong interest in conducting warrantless testing.

It is also clear that the Commission historically has exercised its rulemaking authority in ways that have reduced the justifiable privacy expectations of persons engaged in the horse-racing industry. When jockeys chose to become involved in this pervasively-regulated business and accepted a state license, they did so with the knowledge that the Commission would exercise its authority to assure public confidence in the integrity of the industry. Even before the regulations challenged here were adopted, the jockeys were aware that the Commission had promulgated regulations providing for warrantless searches of stables. In addition, unlike the traditional warrantless search situation, the searches at issue in this case are not unannounced. The jockeys were put on notice that after April 1, 1985 they would be subject to warrantless testing on days that they were engaged to race.

Consequently, while there are distinctions between searches of premises and searches of persons, in the intensely-regulated field of horse racing, where the persons engaged in the regulated activity are the principal regulatory concern, the distinctions are not so significant that warrantless testing for alcohol and drug use can be said to be constitutionally unreasonable. We therefore hold that the administrative search exception applies to warrantless breath and urine testing of employees in the heavily regulated horse-racing industry.[5]

Having determined that the administrative search exception applies to the testing

---

5. Our holding applies only to breathalyzer and urine sampling of voluntary participants in a highly-regulated industry. Thus it should not be read as dispositive of the distinct issue presented in testing of children subject to mandatory school attendance laws or the testing of motor vehicle drivers.

124

of persons engaged in the horse racing industry, there remains the question whether the discretion of the Commission in conducting these searches is sufficiently circumscribed. There is a difference between the manner in which the breathalyzer regulation has been implemented and the manner in which the urine testing regulation has been implemented. Each jockey is required to take a breathalyzer test daily. Thus as this program has been implemented there is no room for standardless discretion. Every jockey knows that an alcohol blood level greater than .05 percent will be detected. The jockeys complain that section 70–14A.10 could be construed to vest standardless discretion in the State Steward, and thus to countenance the abuses anticipated by the Supreme Court in *Marshall v. Barlow's, Inc.*, 436 U.S. 307, 98 S.Ct. 1816, 56 L.Ed.2d 305 (1978). As the district court found, however, as to jockeys it has not been so construed. If it should be, the jockeys are free to return to the district court to litigate that issue.[6]

The urine testing regulation provides that every jockey "may be subjected to a urine test." N.J.Admin.Code tit. 13, § 70–14A.11(b). The trial court found that while all jockeys are at risk of such a test, not all are selected each day. Thus the question presented by the urine testing program as it operates is whether the random selection method is consistent with the requirements of the fourth amendment.

[4] Random searches and seizures that have been held to violate the fourth amendment have left the exercise of discretion as to selected targets in the hands of a field officer with no limiting guidelines. *See, e.g., Delaware v. Prouse*, 440 U.S. 648, 661, 99 S.Ct. 1391, 1400, 59 L.Ed.2d 660 (1979); *United States v. Brignoni-Ponce*, 422 U.S.

873, 882–84, 95 S.Ct. 2574, 2580–82, 45 L.Ed.2d 607 (1975). In the present case the urine tests are mandated by the administrative scheme. The State Steward has no discretion in conducting the tests. Moreover the State Steward has no discretion as to who will be selected for urine testing. That choice is made by a lottery. The determination that a daily program of urine testing at the track, with targets selected randomly, was the most effective means for allocating available resources was made by the Commission, not the field officers. Thus we hold that daily selection by lot of jockeys to be subjected to urine testing does not violate the fourth amendment.[7] *See United States v. Martinez-Fuerte*, 428 U.S. 543, 564–66, 96 S.Ct. 3074, 3085–87, 49 L.Ed.2d 1116 (1976) (holding valid search at checkpoint selected by officials responsible for allocating law enforcement resources).

B. Equal Protection

[5] The jockeys point out that, while all jockeys must submit to a daily breathalyzer test, officials, trainers, and grooms are not subjected to daily testing and that only the jockeys are currently subjected to random selection for the urine testing. Relying on *Yick Wo v. Hopkins*, 118 U.S. 356, 6 S.Ct. 1064, 30 L.Ed. 220 (1886), they contend that such selective enforcement denies jockeys the equal protection of the laws. The district court rejected this contention, relying primarily on the fact that safety concerns are greatest during the running of a race when most serious accidents can occur. The jockeys counter, however, that while this justification may suffice with respect to the breathalyzer tests, it hardly suffices with respect to urine testing, which occurs after the race, not before.

We prefer to rest our affirmance with respect to urine testing on a different

6. This issue would not be foreclosed by our holding that the regulation as applied—requiring all jockeys to submit to a warrantless breathalyzer test on each racing day—does not violate the fourth amendment.

7. To the extent that our holding, that the state may validly seize breath and urine samples from voluntary participants in the regulated

racing industry without a warrant, is inconsistent with the reasoning of *Security and Law Enforcement Employees, Dist. Council 82 v. Carey*, 737 F.2d 187 (2d Cir.1984), we decline to follow that decision. That case held unconstitutional random strip and cavity searches of prison employees for contraband. Choice of targets was not made by lot.

ground. As previously noted, the intense regulation of the racing industry is justified because of public wagering on the outcome of races. Substance abuse by jockeys, who are the most visible human participants in the sport, could affect public confidence in the integrity of that sport. While the state's interest in the appearance of integrity reaches all participants, it is obviously greatest with respect to jockeys. The governing equal protection principle is that the state may rationally take one step at a time. *See, e.g., Williamson v. Lee Optical, Inc.,* 348 U.S. 483, 489, 75 S.Ct. 461, 465, 99 L.Ed. 563 (1955) ("Or the reform may take one step at a time, addressing itself to the phase of the problem which seems most acute to the legislative mind."); *Railway Express Agency, Inc. v. New York,* 336 U.S. 106, 110, 69 S.Ct. 463, 465–66, 93 L.Ed. 533 (1949) ("It is no requirement of equal protection that all evils of the same genus be eradicated or none at all."). Thus we find no merit in the jockeys' equal protection challenge.

C. The Right of Privacy

[6] The jockeys contend that the breathalyzer and urine testing, which involve the collection of medical information, violate their rights of privacy with respect to such information. While both the Supreme Court and this court have recognized a right of privacy in medical information, governmental concerns may support the access to such information where the information is protected from unauthorized disclosure. *See Whalen v. Roe,* 429 U.S. 589, 602, 97 S.Ct. 869, 878, 5 L.Ed.2d 64 (1977); *United States v. Westinghouse Electric Corp.,* 638 F.2d 570, 577 (3d Cir.1980). The Commission's concern for racing integrity justifies its access to the breathalyzer and urinalysis information. The jockeys' concern, therefore, is limited to confidentiality. The jockeys concede that the regulatory amendments concerning confidentiality, proposed while their action was pending and put into effect by the Commission before becoming final, *see* N.J.Admin.Code tit. 13, § 70:14A.11(f) (1985), would satisfy their concerns if the amendments were enforced by an injunction or a declaratory judgment. The district court found no reason to grant declaratory or injunctive relief. We find no abuse of discretion. If the Commission ceases to comply with the proposed confidentiality rules, the jockeys may return to court with a new lawsuit. Their privacy contentions, in the circumstances of this case, are not ripe for adjudication.

Conclusion

We conclude that none of the proffered grounds for reversal of the district court's judgment have merit. The judgment will therefore be affirmed in all respects.